# EVIDENCE GROWTHGUIDE

P9-BYZ-028

# The JOSH McDOWELL TRUTH-ALIVE SERIES

# EVIDENCE GROWTHGUIDE

## Part I

## THE UNIQUENESS OF

## CHRISTIANITY

*Published by*

HERE'S LIFE PUBLISHERS, INC.

San Bernardino, California 92402

EVIDENCE GROWTH GUIDE
PART 1: The Uniqueness of Christianity


A Campus Crusade for Christ Book

Published by
HERE'S LIFE PUBLISHERS, INC.
P. O. Box 1576
San Bernardino, CA 92402


ISBN 0-86605-018-3
HLP Product No. 40-266-9
©Copyright 1981 by Campus Crusade for Christ
All rights reserved.

Printed in the United States of America.

# Table of Contents

# As You Begin

## Why a Growth Guide?

Many Christians have developed confidence in what they believe when they know why they believe it. This Growth Guide will chart a course of discovery for you as you investigate the "why's" of your personal faith in Jesus Christ.

It will help you recognize how your faith is affected by common misconceptions about why we believe, an area in which many fellow believers have nagging questions and doubts.

The entire focus of this Guide is on application, on how evidence for your faith can affect your everyday life and witness. I encourage you to think of this as much more than an academic exercise. Look for ways to translate what you are learning into practical use. Sharing these insights with those in your study group or with your friends and colleagues will help solidify what you learn and will maximize the benefits of the studies.

## Apologize To Whom?

Have you ever been confused by the word "apologetics"? It's understandable if you have. Because of its similarity to "apologize" (which usually means to ask pardon for an offense because we're sorry) the exact meaning of apologetics may elude you.

*apologia*

Technically, the word means to give verbal defense of what a person believes. In Scripture, it simply means to be ready to answer the question, "Why do you believe in Jesus Christ?" It derives its English form from the Greek work *apologia*. It is used eight times in the New Testament and appears in such passages as Acts 22:1, "Brethren and fathers hear my defense *(apologia)* which I now offer to you." It is also used in 1 Peter 3:15, "...be ready always to give an answer *(apologia)*." To be able to present the facts that support a reasonable faith in Jesus Christ as Lord and Savior is an exciting challenge for every Christian.

When you answer a question about why you believe, you engage in apologetics. In other words, apologetics is giving convincing evidence of God's revelation through Jesus Christ. It is important that every believer be equipped to answer questions about *why* he believes.

## Don't Be On The Defensive

I like to say, "The best defense is a good offense." It is so important, whenever we talk to someone, to make the central issue a relationship with Jesus Christ. The purpose of apologetics is not to convince a person, contrary to his will, to become a

Christian. Rather, it is to present the facts of the gospel in the light of Scriptures. Then, after proper reflection and being led by the Holy Spirit, that person can make an intelligent decision for Christ.

Historical evidence of Christianity will never bring a person to a commitment of faith in Jesus Christ. Apologetics never saved anyone. Only the simple message of the gospel has the power to save (Rom. 1:16). That's why I always give just enough apologetics to answer a person's questions and then move ahead to present the gospel.

Apologetics will, however, lay the groundwork for faith. And what a groundwork! Apologetics is not a *substitute* for faith, but a *basis* for it.

It is abundantly clear from Scripture that God the Holy Spirit must be at work before anyone will come to Jesus Christ. One of the tools the Holy Spirit uses is a reasonable explanation of the facts that support the gospel. Therefore, the wise witness will lay those facts before men in such a way as to bring them to the central issue: What will they do with Jesus Christ? That is why I make my message the person of Jesus Christ, not the facts of apologetics. In this way, one can be led to a meaningful and intelligent commitment to Jesus Christ as Lord.

## Be Prepared To Explore

The lessons in this Growth Guide follow a specific format that will help you discover God's truth. The Growth Guide is self-contained and the only other book or material you will need is your Bible. Every lesson contains key Scripture passages to guide you on your exploratory journey into God's Word. We recommend you use the New American Standard Bible.

Each lesson is divided into seven parts. Before you begin the first one, study the following thoroughly. You may also find it helpful to review this explanation as you begin the first few lessons. This will aid in fixing the parts firmly in your mind.

## A Quick Look Back

With the exception of Lesson One, each lesson will begin with a review of the previous lesson, stated in the first person. Make the words your own.

## Key Truth

The primary truth dealt with in the lesson is crystallized, and the learning goals are clearly stated.

## What Would You Say?

Interaction is the keystone of each lesson. Here you have an opportunity to stop, reflect, and reply to a common misconception expressed in conversational style. Consider the conversation to be personally addressed to you. How will you answer?

## Let's Lay A Foundation

The core of each lesson consists of Bible study and basic instruction. Look up each Bible passage referred to and fill in the key words or analyze the passage for its meaning. As you progress through this part of your lesson, keep three major points in mind: (1) Consider. The questions sometimes draw from your present knowledge. Pause and respond to each of these opportunities. It will motivate you to search God's Word. (2) Contemplate. Each lesson is designed to maximize your interaction with God's Word. Allow the Holy Spirit to teach you as you analyze His truth. (3) Comprehend. Be certain you understand the main point before moving on. These lessons are like building blocks. If you miss one of the first blocks, it will be very difficult to fit the others properly into place.

## Feedback

Here is an opportunity to test your comprehension. Without referring to the material you have just covered, try to complete this section. The exercises are both enjoyable and informative. If at the close there are areas you don't recall, don't hesitate to turn to that portion of the lesson and review.

## My Response

Here we share together how God applies the truth to our lives personally. There are three parts: (1) I share how God has made that truth meaningful to me. (2) You are given an opportunity to consider what areas of your life God wants to affect with that same truth. (3) A specific prayer of application summarizes what we have just learned. Identify with each expression and make it your own. Prayerfully consider how God can help you choose to make this true in your life.

## For Further Reference

This section, included in most of the lessons, is provided for those who would like more detailed and documented sources. It will give you the added advantage of reviewing the same material in different form fixing it permanently in mind for later use and sharing. These books are available at your local Christian bookstore or can be obtained by contacting Here's Life Publishers, San Bernardino, CA 92402 (714) 886-7981.

## What's Next?

This volume is called "Evidence Growth Guide, Part I," and is the first in a series of three Growth Guides. The title implies at least two things: (1) the manual provides guidance on how to grow as a Christian; and (2) this growth is based on evidence of the truthfulness of Christianity.

Many would expect a study of evidence that supports the validity of the Christian faith to be boring, an assimilation of dry facts. Nothing could be further from the truth! The vitality of our faith relates directly to the evidence on which Christianity is based. It's our goal to delve deeply into the reasons we base our hopes for eternal salvation on a man—Christ Jesus. What we believe and how we live are intricately linked.

# OUR HOPE

### The Beginning

Imagine this scene. It's 11 P.M. My plane has just landed. I grab my baggage and go outside to wait for my ride home. I'm tired, but confident the car will arrive soon. There's a middle-aged man standing to my right a few paces. Puzzled because I appear so relaxed, he approaches me and asks, "Are you sure your ride will show up?" "Well," I reply, "the driver, whom I know personally, has never failed me. My driver is very safe and punctual, always dependable, and has frequently expressed excitement at having me come home. My *wife* will be here!"

The expectation I express is based upon my confidence in my wife's integrity and trustworthiness. I know her! She's reliable. Actually, the deeper my relationship, the greater my "hope." My "hope" rests on the qualities of the person I trust. To answer why I have hope means I must acquaint someone with my wife's qualities. This is also true of our relationship with Christ.

———————O———————

### Key Truth

*Giving account for the hope I possess as a Christian means acquainting others with the person and character of Christ.*

I will learn

- how my hope is related to my faith.
- how to give an account of my hope in Christ.
- how yielding to Christ's lordship in my life relates to hope.
- how knowing Christ gives me hope.

### What Would You Say?

"Let me ask you. How can you be so happy? Look at all the problems of the world: pollution, food and energy shortages, overpopulation, war and the potential of a nuclear holocaust! How can you be optimistic? I think happiness is what I can find today, in the present. Life is now and I must get from it all I can. Tomorrow is so uncertain. . ."

What would *you* say?

I would say _to see what's happening in the world only, makes it clear in my mind that Christ is the answer — He predicted all this in the Bible._

Because _____

—It's _not God's doing. → But man's own will + pride ⇒ contrary to God's original plan_

———————○———————

## Let's Lay A Foundation

### I. The hope we have.

The Bible has a great deal to say about hope. One significant passage relates directly to the hope we have as believers in Christ and the answer we are to give when called upon to account for that hope. It is found in 1 Peter 3:15. (Fill in the missing words.)

"...but sanctify Christ as Lord in your hearts, _always being ready_ to make a defense to every one who asks you to _about the hope that is with in you_ yet with _gentleness + reverence_ ..."

There are three clear implications from this passage.

1. Give a reason.

As believers we must be prepared to explain the reason for our hope in this life.

Peter assumes that inquiries will come, not because unbelievers are curious about why we're Christians, but because they sense a quality about our lifestyle. The question is, "What is the reason for your joyful optimism? How can you be so certain about life?" We answer with a positive declaration as to why we trust Christ!

2. Be hopeful.

Faith brings hope for the future. When I'm called upon to account for why I have hope in this life, I present the reasons I trust Christ the way I do. To answer why I have hope in Christ is to explain why I am confident He is worthy of my trust.

This is how faith and hope relate. We have hope because of our faith in Christ who always keeps His word.

My Faith

My Hope

The Trustworthiness of Christ

3. Share it in love.

We should be able to share why we have hope in an unruffled, respectful manner ("with gentleness and reverence"). It is the quiet, dynamic influence of our life that has the greatest impact.

Now, describe your understanding of hope and faith.

(1) What does hope mean to you?  *now/*

*— confidence in future*
*what Christ says about the future.*

(2) Describe faith as you now understand it.

*it's not so much How much faith I have → It's the object of my faith*

## II. The tests we face.

Scripture tells us we are blessed when we suffer unjustly. That's hard to swallow. Yet the tests we endure largely determine the depth and scope of our hope. We are equipped to answer concerning our hope through testing.

Evaluate the context of the Key Verse, 1 Peter 3:15. Do so by completing these neighboring verses.

Vs. 9: "not returning _____*evil*_____ for _____*evil*_____, or _____*insult*_____ for _____*insult*_____, but giving _____*a blessing*_____ _____*instead.*_____ for you were called for the very purpose that _____*you might inherit*_____ _____*a blessing*_____."

13

Vs. 14: "But even if you should _suffer for the sake_ _righteousness_____, you are blessed. And do not fear

✳ _their intimidation_ and _do not be troubled._"

Vs. 16: "And _keep a good conscience_____ so that in the thing in which you are slandered, those who revile your _good_____ _behaviour in Christ_____ may be put to shame."

Vs. 17: "For it is better, if God should will it so, that you suffer for _doing_____ _what is right_____ rather than for _what is not right._____."

Significantly, it is in the context of suffering that we are commanded to set Christ up as Lord of our lives. This is the secret to courage and success in facing opposition. Often, we wrongly focus on how this suffering can build us. Instead we should consider how this problem tests our confidence in a sovereign Christ who controls our lives.

When faced by trying circumstances or temptation, I used to ask quickly, "Lord, what area of my character do you wish to build?" or "What lesson is in this for me?" I thought troublesome circumstances were somehow designed to build me, to make me a better Christian, but I soon learned those were the wrong questions. Trials were not designed to test my character. God tempts no one (James 1:13). Trials simply provide me with an opportunity to rely on and trust in Christ's sovereign control.

I now have a bright prospect of hope for even the most worrisome trial. I know the outcome is not up to me. And it's not necessary to focus on some quality that's lacking in my life. Trials increase my hope and build my character as a *result* of trusting Christ in *that* situation.

**III. The Lord we serve.**

Note the first phrase of 1 Peter 3:15.

"...but _Sanctify Christ as Lord in your hearts_ always being ready..."

In your opinion, what significance does this have in giving account for the hope we have in Christ?

_we have no hope — if Christ_ _is not Lord in our hearts_

_____

14

Who is able to proclaim Christ as Lord?

1 Corinthians 12:3— *those who speak by the Holy Spirit*

When I submit myself to Christ's control and lordship, I place my confidence in His ability to manage the affairs of my life. And that brings hope!

I now have an assured expectation that Christ will fulfill His predestined plan for me. The master controller is at the controls of my life!

The deeper my relationship, the greater my hope. As I come to know Him better I get a clearer view of His qualities and qualifications. Remember, having hope depends upon the qualities of the person I trust. The less I know those qualities, the less confident will be my expectations.

## Conclusion

A deepening and growing relationship with Christ relates directly to my ability to give an answer as to why I have hope. Knowing *why* I believe specifically increases my faith in Christ.

As a believer, I will be asked, "What causes you to be so joyful and optimistic?" My faith relationship with Jesus Christ, based on facts about His person and work, will enable me to give a meaningful reply.

This Growth Guide strengthens our faith relationship with Jesus Christ by focusing on five aspects of His character. This will help us to know Him better. I have discovered that underlying any misconception of Christianity is a misunderstanding about Christ. Therefore we will expose five misconceptions about the Christian faith by studying what God's word teaches us about Christ. For each misconception there is a corresponding truth about Christ. By knowing him better, all of our intellectual, moral, social and spiritual needs will be met.

| MISCONCEPTION | TRUTH ABOUT CHRIST | RESPONSE |
|---|---|---|
| I. Christianity is a system of beliefs. | He is my authority. | I follow Him. |
| II. The Christian's faith is a subjective faith. | He is my righteousness. | I live through Him. |
| III. The Christian's faith is a blind faith. | He is my ultimate resource. | I receive from Him. |
| IV. The Christian's faith has no historical basis. | He is my wisdom. | I perceive through Him. |
| V. Christianity cannot be proven. | He is my controller. | I am directed by Him. |

*scientifically*

*historical*

15

Without referring to the lesson, complete these multiple choice questions (A or B):

__B__ 1. I am joyfully optimistic about the future because of my faith in:

   (A) mankind's ability to achieve peace and prosperity.

   (B) Christ's ability to bring all things into subjection to Himself.

__A__ 2. When I face trials, this tests:

   (A) my faith in who and what Christ is.

   (B) my character, so I can grow spiritually.

__B__ 3. My hope for the future depends upon:

   (A) how much I believe.

   (B) the qualities of the person I trust.

__B__ 4. Knowing *why* I believe is important because:

   (A) it helps me convince others that what I believe is true.

   (B) it teaches me the reasons Christ is worthy of my trust.

Taking into account Hebrews 11:1, what is your definition of faith?

*- the assurance of things hoped for*
*- the conviction of things not seen*

Compose a concise definition of hope.

*Hope* → *belief that my future is secure based on the qualities of Christ*

––––––––––––––––––––o––––––––––––––

*Josh*

Before I met Christ, happiness depended upon favorable circumstances, and hope for a better life rested in my ability to change the unfavorable circumstances. I was seldom happy then, because so often I could neither control myself nor change my environment. However, now that I know Christ, my hope rests in His ability to control all things, and the better I know Him, the greater confidence I have about my future.

As parents, Dottie and I have wondered about our children's future, but we have gained contentment about their uncertain tomorrows as our confidence has grown in Christ, the one who holds the future.

_Judi Johnston_ +
(My name)

What characteristics make Christ worthy of my trust?

→ faithfulness * - His self sacrificing love for me.
→ the truth
→ righteousness    - d

Therefore, I will trust Christ for the following areas of my life:

- my education
- my rel'p w Jim (or whoever God has for me!)
- my career.
- my friends. my family.

I will make this prayer my own:

> "Lord Jesus, I thank You for being worthy of my trust. Faith in You brings me hope because I know You are in control of my life. I reaffirm my commitment to Your Lordship. I want to know You better, for I know that my relationship with You is the basis for the confident expectation I have for the future. Amen."

———————O———————

## For Further Reference

On "What hope does Christianity offer the world?", read _Answers to Tough Questions_ pages 121-122.

Donna Kaye
+ Linda Krepp
Tammy Link

# Misconception No. 1

# CHRISTIANITY IS A SYSTEM
# OF BELIEFS

# CHRIST IS A PERSON

### A Quick Look Back

I am beginning to understand that my "hope" is directly related to how well I know Jesus. The buoyant, confident way I face life, even with its troubles, is based on how well I know Christ. The better I know Him, the greater my hope. Giving someone an account for my hope means acquainting him with the qualifications of the person I trust!

### Key Truth

**A Christian's faith is in a person, not a set of beliefs.**

I will learn:

- that Christianity is different from all religions.
- that Christianity is based upon the person of Christ, and not just His teachings.
- that Jesus made His identity the central issue.
- that Christianity is a relationship, and not a religion.

### What Would You Say?

"Essentially, all religions are alike, with only minor differences. They all teach, 'love your neighbor, be good, don't steal, don't kill, don't cheat, be kind and make the world a better place.' Take Christianity, for instance. Christ taught that we should follow the Golden Rule by being kind to our neighbors.

"So I say religion is like choosing a car. There are lots of models and makes, but they're all designed to get you where you want to go. Whether it's Buddha, Mohammed, Moses or Christ, they all teach the same thing, they all go the same place..."

What would you say? "I dont know" Amnew

I would say Christ is God in flesh — others were mere men — he came to make us able to know God — not just as a good man

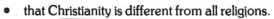

Because _____

_____

_____

—————————○—————————

## Let's Lay A Foundation

### I. Christianity *is* Christ.

I used to consider Christianity's teachings as its most important feature. I thought if I could prove them false, I could expose Christianity as a fraud. However, as I investigated historical, biblical Christianity, I came face to face with Jesus Christ and His claims. I then realized that Christianity is not just a set of abstract beliefs but a relationship with a person.

I discovered that Christianity is based on the life, character, death and resurrection of Jesus Christ. So, instead of learning that Christ came to *teach* Christianity, I realized that Christ *is* Christianity.

Most other religions are based on philosophical propositions or theological ideologies. Remove the founding prophet or guru, and the religion remains essentially intact.

#### 1. Mohammed

KORAN

Remove Mohammed from Islam, and Islam remains. Mohammed, being simply the communicator of Allah's will, is not critically important to Islam; but what he communicated about Allah and his will is all-important to that religion. In Islam, then, the message is far more important than the founding messenger. The teachings count for more than the teacher!

#### 2. Buddha

Remove Buddha, and Buddhism remains. Buddhism rests mainly on Buddha's teachings, which instruct the faithful to lead a tranquil life through attainment of a disciplined state of mind. Buddha, himself, is not essential to the quest.

*ή ἁμαρτία*

### 3. Confucius

Remove Confucius, and Confucianism remains. Confucianism teaches philosophical concepts about wise behavior. It is a religion in which the identity of Confucius, its founder, is inconsequential.

THE PERSON OF CHRIST

### 4. Christ (No Christ—No Christianity)

Remove Christ, however, and Christianity crumbles. The identity of Jesus is crucial to Christianity. Without Christ, Christianity would cease to exist, for it rests upon His claim to be the eternal Son of God, a claim attested to by the resurrection.

## II. Jesus is a person.

1. The great confession. (Read Matthew 16:13-20.)

What essential question did Jesus ask His disciples?

Vs. 13 *who do men say I am?*
*who do (you) say I am?*

What were the popular opinions concerning Jesus' identity?

Vs. 14 *— John the B., Elias, Jeremias a prophet*

Who did Peter say Jesus was?

Vs. 16 *The Christ, the Son of the living God!*

Did Jesus commend or rebuke Peter? Explain.

Vs. 17 _commended him — for it was Jesus' father who revealed it to him._

Since the validity and significance of all that Christ taught depends on *who* He is, He asked, "Who do you say that I am?" Interestingly, He never asked for an opinion about His teachings.

2. The "I" of the gospel.

While other religious teachers put their teachings out front and themselves in the background, Jesus put Himself out front, speaking of Himself in an extraordinary fashion and making His identity the focus of His teachings.

What did Jesus say about Himself?

(1) "I am _that bread of life_" (John 6:48).

The Jews considered bread to be essential for sustaining life. With this in mind, explain Jesus' claim.

_You can have no life wout me —_

(2) "I am _the door_" (John 10:9).

In view of the Jews' familiarity with sheep and shepherding, what do you suppose they understood from Jesus' teaching?

_he is our protection — he provides entrance to s.t. (unique)_

How does Jesus refer to Himself in John 10:14? Does this differ from Jesus' claim to be "the door"?

_I am good shepherd —_

*KEY*

(3) In what four ways does Jesus identify Himself in John 14:6?

I am _____way_____ ,

and _____truth_____ ,

and _____life_____ ;

no one comes to the Father,

but _____by ME_____ .

Jesus did not claim to know the way; He *was* the way. He did not say He would teach the truth; He *was* the truth. He did not say He would explain a way of life; He *was* the life. He did not promise to explain the way to God; He was (and is) the way to God.

III. **Christianity is a relationship.**    *sinful man*    *Jesus*    *Holy God*

The gospel story tells how sinful man can have fellowship with a Holy God through faith in Jesus Christ, the one who died for our sins and rose from the dead. When anyone trusts in Christ, he enters into a right relationship with God. Christianity, then, is primarily a relationship.

Identify the kinds of relationships you find in these verses:

Genesis 3:8— _____broken_____

Mark 3:14— _____teacher_____

1 Corinthians 1:9— _____fellowship (friends)_____

Hebrews 4:15— _____empathizer_____

Revelation 3:20— _____understanding/acceptance_____

God created man and woman for fellowship with Him, but they rejected His fellowship and chose to rebel (sin). Subsequently, all have sinned, but God had determined to restore us to Himself. The plan called for Jesus, God the Son, to become the God-man and die on the cross, suffering the penalty of sin on our behalf. The plan was carried out and God's righteous justice was satisfied. Now God is able to bring us into loving fellowship with Himself as His forgiven children.

That's the gospel: God reaching down to us, offering us a relationship with Himself through Christ. Religion, by contrast, is man's attempt to reach God, an attempt that always fails.

## Conclusion

Christianity is not based on its ethical teachings or doctrinal concepts but on Jesus Christ, whereas most religions are based on philosophical propositions or theological ideologies. If you remove the founding prophet or guru from any of these religions, they remain essentially the same. But if you remove Christ from Christianity, you simply have no Christianity, for Christ *is* Christianity. Personal faith in Christ establishes a relationship with God, thereby distinguishing Christianity from all other religions.

---○---

## Feedback

Do you *agree* or *disagree* with these statements? (Mark A or D)

___A___1. Christianity is based on the life, character, death and resurrection of its founder, Jesus Christ.

___A___2. Religion is man's attempt to reach God, whereas Christianity is God reaching out to man.

___A___3. Other religions are based on philosophical propositions or theological ideologies. Remove the founding prophet or guru, and the religion remains the same.

___A___4. Having a personal relationship with God by faith distinguishes Christianity from all other religions.

___D___5. Jesus was primarily concerned with people's opinion of His teachings.

---○---

## My Response

### Josh

As a university student, I was challenged by a group of Christians to investigate the truthfulness of Christianity. Not long after I met these Christians, I learned something that altered my outlook on Christianity. I asked one of the students, "Tell me, what changed your life?" She said, "Jesus Christ." I never thought I'd hear *that* in the university. I said, "Don't feed me that garbage; I'm fed up with religion." She shot

26

back, "Mister, I didn't say religion; I said the person of Jesus Christ." Her reply pointed out something I'd never known before—Christianity is not a religion; it's a relationship which God is offering men and women through his Son, Jesus Christ.

_Judy Johnston_ _Vivian Zeung_ 汪依文
(My name)

**In what specific ways am I cultivating my relationship with God?**

_tsun hai ? !_
_Really ._

_prayer._ — _in trouble_
— _thankful._

_read His word — the Bible_

**What hindrances will I face in fulfilling my commitment?**

_CHOICE_

_laziness_
_business_
_absent minded_

_.. organize my schedule._
_— priorities_ _5mn / am._

**In seeking a more dynamic personal relationship, I will make this prayer my own:**

"Lord Jesus, I want to know You more fully as the person You are. I know I sometimes live the Christian life as if it depended upon following rules rather than cultivating a relationship with You. I thank You for being the person You are. Right now help me to understand the meaning of Your friendship. I purpose to know You better. Amen."

_* choice_

———————————o———————————

## For Further Reference

For a fuller explanation of God's redemptive plan, read chapter 10, "Isn't there some other way?" in _More Than A Carpenter_, pages 111-116.

To examine the difference between Christianity and other religions, read the section, "World Religions," in _Answers to Tough Questions_, pages 108-118. Also read "Why is Jesus the only way to get to God?" pages 62-64.

# CHRIST HAS A POSITION

### A Quick Look Back

I have discovered that Christianity is a relationship with a person, Jesus Christ. This makes Christianity different from all other religions.

———————————————○———————————————

### Key Truth

*The deity of Christ is essential to the Christian's faith.*

I will learn:

1. • of Christ's claims to be God. $X = G$ , $X$ is called $G$
2. • of Christ's authority over all things.
3. • of Christ's authority to forgive sins. $X$ as $G$ forgives sins

———————————————○———————————————

### What Would You Say?

"I think it's admirable that you believe in Jesus Christ as your Savior. But remember, Jesus never claimed to be God. He referred to Himself as the 'Son of Man' but not as the 'Son of God.' He died as a martyr for His beliefs; and I admire Him for that, but it was His followers who made Him into a God and made a religion out of it!"

What would *you* say?

I would say _____

_____

_____

Because _____

_____

_____

———————————○———————————

## Let's Lay A Foundation

If I place my faith in someone who is unworthy of my trust, my faith is hopeless and empty. So it is important to ask, "Who is Jesus Christ? Is He worthy of my trust?" After all, IF JESUS IS NOT GOD, THEN HE IS UNABLE TO FULFILL THE HOPE ON WHICH MY FAITH IS BASED. So I need to know if Christ's claims to be God are valid.

### I. Christ is equal with God. (Read John 5:17,18.)

Jesus called God "My Father" when He answered the venemous criticism of the Jews over His healing a lame man on the Sabbath. He said, "My Father is working until now, and I Myself am working" (verse 17).

*calling God his own Father.*

What was the Jews' reaction?

Vs. 18 *they tried harder to kill him —plotting*

_____

What major claim did Jesus make that made the Jews so murderously angry?

Vs. 18 *— he was the Son of God ∴ = to God.*

_____

Explain why the Jews interpreted Jesus calling God "My Father" as making Himself equal with God?

_____

_____

_____

By calling God His Father, Jesus clearly established two main points about Himself.

   (1) He equated *His* work with the work of *God, the Father* (verse 17).

   (2) He claimed equality with God by saying, "My Father," for Jews never referred to God as "My Father." They would say, "Our Father," and qualify this with "in heaven."

29

## II. Christ is called God. (Read John 8:48-59.)

Jesus called Himself "I Am," a name which signifies God's eternal existence. It was not an unfamiliar name to the Jews, because it appears in the Old Testament. Read the following Scriptures and identify the one with whom the Jews would associate this name.

Exodus 3:14 _God said to Moses — to say "I am" has sent me."_

Deuteronomy 32:39 _there is No God beside me "I myself am he" < source of life_

Isaiah 43:10 _I am He — "No God before me or after me" + death_

Why, then, did these Jewish leaders respond so negatively?

_____

_____

_____

_Anyone who blasphemes the name must be stoned._

Because Jesus identified Himself as the eternal Jehovah of the Old Testament, the Jews picked up stones to throw at Him. They felt He was guilty of blasphemy and therefore must be stoned to death in accordance with the teaching of Leviticus 24:16. Obviously these Jews, strict in observing the law, had not missed the meaning of Jesus' claim.

## III. Christ, as God, forgives sin. (Read Mark 2:5-12.)

When Jesus said, "My son, your sins are forgiven," the scribes immediately caught the implication of His words. What was their response?

(Vs. 6,7) "But there are some of the scribes sitting there and reasoning in their hearts, 'Why does this man speak that way?'

_He's blaspheming_ ; _Who can forgive sins but God Alone?_ ?'"

Jesus' reply to this challenge may seem puzzling at first glance.

(Vs. 9,10) " 'Which is easier, to say to the paralytic,

" _Your sins are forgiven_ "; or to say,

" _Get up! Take your mat + walk._ ?" But in order that you may know that the Son of Man has authority on earth to forgive sins,' He said to the paralytic,

30

G.

*I tell you — get up! Take up your bed + go home ..."*

What becomes increasingly clear, as you ponder the meaning of this passage, is the impact of Jesus' claim to forgive sins. How can a mere man forgive sins committed against God? And how can such a claim be verified?

By healing the sick man, Jesus demonstrated His authority and His ability to forgive sin. He certified what could not be seen (the forgiving of sins) by what could be seen (the healing of the sick man). Only God can forgive sins *committed* against God, and only God can heal bodies originally *created* by God.

**IV.** **Christ was tried for being God. (Read Mark 14:60-64.)** the Jews understood his claim to be God!

"Are You the Christ?" This question, asked by the high priest at Jesus' trial, was one of the most obvious indications that the Jews understood Jesus' claim to be God.

Christ's testimony before the high priest shows that He claimed to be:

(1) (vs. 61) The Son of _the Blessed One_ (God).

(2) (vs. 62) One who would sit _at the Rt hand of the Mighty One_

(3) (vs. 62) The Son of Man who would come _on the clouds_ _of Heaven)_ .

Christ's threefold testimony stunned his accusers. Why did the high priest tear his clothes?

Vs. 63,64 _Why do we Need witnesses? Blasphemy!!_

What was the verdict?

Vs. 64 _Condemned to (death) —spit → beat ū fists_

The charges at Christ's trial centered on His true identity. In most trials, defendants are tried for what they have done. But Jesus of Nazareth was sentenced to death because of *who* He was, not for *what* He had done.

### Conclusion

Jesus' claim to deity was recognized clearly by the Jewish leaders, but they regarded it as blasphemy and demanded that He be crucified because "He made Himself out to be the Son of God." So Jesus was rejected because of who He was—the God-man. Men do not reject Him today because of His teachings. He is rejected because of His claim to be Lord of their lives. As God, Jesus has full authority to forgive every one of our sins!

*Yahweh*

Without referring to the material you have just covered, show that you understand the significance of Christ's claims about Himself by completing the following sentences. Check your answers with the key at the close of this lesson.

1. At the trial of Jesus, the high priest tore his clothes, because he felt Jesus was guilty of _Blasphemy_.

2. "I and My Father _are one_."

3. Jesus identified Himself as the _eternal Johovah._ "I Am" of the Old Testament.

4. Christ was tried because of _who he was_, not _what he'd done_.

True or False:

__T__1. The charges at Christ's trial centered on His true identity.

__T__2. The identity of Jesus Christ as God is critical to the meaning of faith.

__F__3. Jews frequently referred to God as "My Father." ✗ our father

__T__4. The "I Am" of John 8:58 is the name God used in revealing Himself to Moses in the burning bush.

__T__5. Jesus' claim to forgive sins is an unmistakable claim to deity. Only God can forgive sins committed against God.

———————○———————

Josh

As I have shared Christ, I have found very few people with real intellectual problems regarding Christianity. Many have intellectual excuses though. For the most part, they reject Christ, not because of His teachings but because He demands the final authority over their lives. Knowing this, I often share that Christ is the most loving and kind "authority figure" they could ever imagine, and I tell them that accepting Christ starts a wonderful growing relationship with our creator God. I point out that, because of His position as God, Jesus has the power to forgive every sin I commit. That's a friend worth having!

32

_____

*Judi Nhe* (signature)

(My name)

Marginal notes (top right):
- future
- career
- rel'p u Michl
- school /studies
- sky + family

**How does Jesus' position of (authority) relate to me right now?** sky + family

Because (of His authority) → I must allow Him to be Lord of every area of my life

**One fact I never knew before about Christ's deity is:** _____

As God, Christ has authority to ~~Committed~~ forgive sins comm. contre Dieu.

**My hope in Christ has been deepened by:** _____

the confidence we can have in Christ — knowing he IS GOD ... not just another religious leader

I will make the words of this prayer my own:

> "Lord Jesus, I am amazed that I have the honor of knowing You personally. You are in the position of final authority over all things. Most importantly, because of Your position as God, You are able to forgive my sins. Thank You for Your forgiveness. Amen."

————————O————————

## For Further Reference

For an in-depth review of Christ's claims to be God, read chapter 6 of *Evidence That Demands a Verdict*, pages 89-102.

Christ's claim to be God make Him distinct from all religious leaders. Read chapter 1 of *More Than a Carpenter*, pages 9-24, to examine what makes Jesus so different.

"Did Jesus claim to be God?" Read pages 39-41 of *Answers to Tough Questions* for a concise answer to this crucial question.

KEY
Fill-in Questions: 1. blasphemy; 2. are one; 3. eternal Jehovah;
4. who He was, what He had done.
True or False: 1. True 2. True 3. False 4. True 5. True

# CHRIST IS MY PROVIDER/PROTECTOR

## A Quick Look Back

I have learned that the central issue in Christianity is the identity of Christ. If He is not God, then my trust in Him is empty and vain, for He would not be able to reward my hope in Him. But I have seen that Christ unmistakably made clear His claim to be God. He is equal with God. He bears the same name as God. He is of the same nature as God. He forgives sin, and He professed openly at His trial His identity as God. Because of *who* He was, and not because of what He taught or did, His opponents crucified Him.

---○---

## Key Truth

*By accepting God's provisions and protection, I am free to accept others unconditionally.*

I will learn:

- that Christ has God's authority.
- that Christ desires to provide all needs.
- that Christ wishes to protect His people from the evil consequences of sin.
- how we are able to accept others unconditionally.

## What Would You Say?

"We were made with basic needs, desires and drives which must be fulfilled through interpersonal relationships in which there is a give and take 50/50 proposition. I give 50 percent, you give 50 percent! In these relationships, equality is crucial, for problems occur when one person is not willing to give his part. Besides, I need self fulfillment. I need to keep 50 percent for myself so I can grow as a person..."

What would *you* say?

I would say ___That's an interesting way to put it.___
___I always thought it was a 100/100___
___prop.___

34

Because _Because all intra personal relationships_ _are based on "love" and "love" requires nothing_ _in return therefore no need to keep 50%._ _? no need to ask 50% of the person._

---○---

## Let's Lay A Foundation

How does Christ being God practically affect my interpersonal relationships? For every truth given in the Bible about God, there is a corresponding practical application. Truths *about* Christ have a direct bearing on my relationship *with* Him.

### I. Christ is the *authority* of God.

It's exciting to realize that Christ, being in the position of God, has the authority of God.

In fact, everything that can be said of God can also be said of Christ. Since Christ is truly God, *He* is everything *God* is. At first this may not appear to be an earth-shaking idea, but think about it a moment. Because Christ is God, He has total authority and control over all things.

1. Christ proclaimed His authority.

In delegating the responsibility of world evangelism to His disciples, Jesus declared His authority.

"And Jesus came up and spoke to them, saying, _all authority in_ _Heaven & Earth_ has been given to Me _therefore go &_ _make disciples -_ ..." (Matthew 28:18).

2. God will proclaim Christ's authority.

Because Christ is God's Son, God the Father will declare His Son's authority.

"Have this attitude in yourselves which was also in Christ Jesus, who,

although _being in the form of God_

did not regard _equality w/ God something to be_ _grasped_

a thing to be grasped" (Phillipians 2:5,6).

"Therefore also God highly exalted Him, and bestowed on Him _a_ _name which is above every name._ that at the name of Jesus _every knee should bow_.

35

of those who are in heaven, and on earth...and that _every_

_tongue should confess that_

_Jesus Christ is Lord_ ,

to the glory of God the Father" (Philippians 2:9-11).

3. God's Word proclaims Christ's authority.

As God incarnate, Christ exercises complete authority over all.

"For in Him _all fulness of the Deity is in him_

in bodily form, and in Him you have been made complete, and He is the

_head_ over all rule and authority" (Colossians 2:9,10).

## II. Christ is the *love* of God.

This is the second truth *about* Christ that affects my relationship *with* Him. It is Christ's loving purpose to meet every need we may have.

Many people dislike authority because of its prohibitions, yet many don't realize that behind every negative command there are two positive principles. Christ wishes to *protect* us and to *provide* for us. What motivation this gives!

My faith and hope in Christ are based on a confident expectation that, because of who He is (my personal provider and protector) He will always care for me and my needs.

1. King David's testimony.

What characteristics of God's loving protection and provision do you find in Psalms 145:14-20?

_Protection_ (vs. 14)—"The Lord _upholds all those who fall_ ,

And _lifts up_ all who are _bowed down_ ."

_Provision_ (vs. 15,16)—"The eyes of all _look to you_ ,

And Thou dost _give them their food_ in due time.

Thou dost _open your hand and satisfy desires_
_of every living thing_ "

_Protection_ (vs. 18)—"The Lord _is near to all who call_ .

upon Him, To all who call upon Him in truth."

_Provision_ (vs. 19)—"He will _fulfill desires of_

of those who fear Him."

_Protection_ (vs. 19,20) — "He will also hear their cry _and save them._

_____. The Lord _watches over all._

who love Him "

2. King David's experience.

How did God wish to demonstrate His loving provision and protection to King David? Read 2 Samuel 12:1-15 and respond to the following:

Who confronted David with the enormity of his sin?

_Nathan_

How had God provided for David in the past?

Vs. 7,8— _gave him everything he desired. Made King - saved from Saul - master's house - master's wives all house of Israel & Judah_

By defining "despised" (vs. 9), describe David's response to God's provision.

_He had Uriah killed in battle and took his wife._

What were some consequences of David's sin that God could have protected him from?

Vs. 10,11— ~~stopped~~ _prevented the pregnancy. allowed baby to live & Scheming could have worked and Uriah slept w/ his wife._

In this incident, King David illustrates the tragic results of failing to trust God as provider. The consequences of his sin were precisely what God had wished to protect him from. If only God is to meet my needs, my total expectation should be in Him. King David learned this lesson the hard way when he took it upon himself to provide for his own needs instead of trusting in God.

By refusing to submit to God's authority and trust Him for all his needs, David took matters into his own hands and denied God's ability to provide and protect.

When we determine where and when we will accept God's provisions, we deny our faith in Him as the only one who desires to meet all our needs.

## III. Christ is the *power* of God.

This is such a commonly accepted fact that its import eludes us. Because Christ is the power of God, He has the infinite capacity to fulfill every need. Therefore, my expectations must be in Christ, not in those around me. He is the only one able to meet my needs. These are not empty promises. Christ has the power to make His promises good!

"Do not be deceived, my beloved brethren.

_____ *every good gift* _____ and _____ *every perfect gift* _____ is from above, coming down from the Father of lights, with whom there is no variation, or shifting shadow" (James 1:16,17).

"Do not be anxious then, saying, 'What shall we eat?' or 'What shall we drink?' or 'With what shall we clothe ourselves?' For all these things the Gentiles eagerly seek; for your heavenly Father knows _____

_____ *your every need* _____ . But seek first His

kingdom, and His righteousness; and all these things _____ *shall be*

_____ *given to you* _____ " (Matthew 6:31-33).

"If you then, being evil, know how to give good gifts to your children, _____

_____ *how much more then will your father* who is in

heaven *give good gifts* _____ to those who ask Him!"

(Matthew 7:11)

"And my God _____ *shall supply all your needs*

according to _____ *his riches in glory* _____ in Christ

Jesus" (Philippians 4:19).

## Conclusion

Christ is the authority, love and power of God. Therefore:

1. I will put my expectations in God alone.

I'm encouraged and rewarded when I focus my expectations in God as being totally capable of meeting my needs. However, my faith is frequently put to the test. Because I can't see God actively at work, I am often tempted to believe that my provisions come from myself or others. So I constantly need to recall from Scripture that God alone is the ultimate source of provision for all my needs.

2. I will release others from binding expectations.

When I place my expectations in God alone, I release those closest to me from stifling expectations. I recognize they are not the source of supply and, therefore, are not responsible for providing for me. And, by not shackling others by my demands, I create an atmosphere that motivates them to be used by God to respond to my needs.

3. I will learn to accept God's provisions through others.

When I expect from God, this does not keep God from providing through others to meet my needs. In fact, God *does* choose to work through others. In accepting God's choices for meeting my needs, I am able to develop close relationships with others, for I view them as an integral part of God's plan for me.

This perspective is liberating in two ways: 1) I am free from my attachment to myself and others, for I no longer depend upon myself or others as a source of fulfillment; and 2) those closest to me are extremely motivated to change for the better, since I accept them for what they are.

———————O———————

## Feedback

Decide whether you *agree* or *disagree*. (Mark A or D.)

_____1. It is important to recognize that Christ alone is able to meet all my needs.

_____2. Christ is dependent on others for meeting my needs.

_____3. My expectation should be in Christ so that I can accept His protection and provision through others.

_____4. Accepting Christ as authority (Provider and Protector) causes me to make demands on others.

_____5. The only way I can develop proper relationships with others is by developing a proper relationship with Christ.

———————O———————

## My Response

*Josh*

Knowing Christ as God in the position of authority has drastically affected my personal relationships. I used to think that, if I accepted Dottie (my wife) just as she was, she would never change for the better and she would not be able to meet my needs as God designed. Was I wrong! For me, knowing Christ as Provider and

Protector has made me realize that Dottie does not meet my needs—Christ does. I simply accept His provisions through my wife and accept her for what she is, without expecting or demanding that she change. Dottie, too, has come to accept me in the same way. Her unconditional acceptance creates in me a natural response to be the kind of person she knows I ought to be. The atmosphere of acceptance evokes the attitude of love.

_____

(My name)

In what specific areas of my life can I praise God for being my Provider and Protector?

_____

_____

_____

Who closest to me is God using to provide for me?

_____

_____

_____

What consequences of sin does God wish to protect me from today, as I choose to obey Him?

_____

_____

_____

I will affirm Christ's authority over me by praying:

> "Lord Jesus, I praise You for Your personal regard for my needs. I acknowledge You as final authority over my life, and I rejoice in the provision and protection You give me. Help me to look only to You to fulfill all my needs. I place my expectation in You as the sufficient provider and protector of my life. Amen."

————————O————————

## For Further Reference

The principles discussed in this lesson can equally be applied to love, sex and marriage. Read *Givers, Takers and Other Kinds of Lovers*, chapters 4 and 5, pages 37-65.

# Misconception No. 2

## THE CHRISTIAN'S FAITH IS
## A SUBJECTIVE FAITH

# CHRIST IS THE OBJECT OF FAITH

### A Quick Look Back

I've learned that because Christ is God He is able to fulfill the promise of my hope in Him. As God, He has the authority and power to accomplish His will in my life. In His position of ultimate authority, He has the ability to fulfill all my expectations. Even His negative commands are reinforced by two positive goals. He wants to: 1) provide for me, and 2) protect me. I can safely trust in Christ, knowing He will grant what is best.

---○---

### Key Truth

**The Christian's faith finds its worth in the object in which it's placed.**

I will learn:

- that faith has no value in itself.
- that faith finds its value in the object in which it's placed.
- that Christ is the object of the Christian's faith.
- that salvation is *by* grace *through* faith *in* Jesus.

### What Would You Say?

"The most important thing in religion is to believe. And that's great! Everyone needs something to believe in. I admire people like you who believe enough to devote a lifetime to it. So, if Christ is good for you, hang in there, but I don't think it makes any difference what you believe in. The important thing is that we all *believe*..."

What would *you* say?

I would say _____

_____

_____

Because _____

_____

Many in society consider faith to be entirely subjective. They feel that if religion meets essential needs, it's fine to believe it. According to this approach, it doesn't matter what you believe, as long as you believe it sincerely.

As I began to investigate biblical Christianity, I discovered that true faith is objective. It must have an object.

### I.  Faith in itself has no value.

Faith is not some magic formula, insuring salvation for the person who possesses it. Faith is trust, and it acts like an arm reaching out to receive what Christ offers.

Every person has the capability to trust because it's part of our makeup as creatures who reflect the image of our Creator. We all exercise a kind of faith from the moment we get up in the morning until we turn in at night. (Even lying in bed requires faith!) If we did not exercise some type of faith, our lives would be chaotic. But that kind of faith can't save us or bring us into a right relationship with God, because it doesn't rest in the right object.

It is the Holy Spirit who shows men and women that Christ is the only worthy object of faith. Someone even may believe sincerely in another god or religion, but his faith won't save him. *A person can be sincere, but sincerely wrong!* Sincerity is not enough if the object is untrustworthy.

### II.  Faith in an object has value.

Since faith has no value in itself, it must find its worth in the object in which it's placed. This is objective faith. If the object is trustworthy, faith is vindicated, but if the object proves untrustworthy, faith is useless.

Since Christ is the object of the Christian's faith, that faith is valuable because Christ is trustworthy. The value of faith is not *in the one believing* but rather in *the one who is believed*. What counts, then, is not the faithfulness of the one believing but the faithfulness of the one who is believed. Christ, being the object of the Christian's faith, has all the qualities necessary to make that faith of infinite value.

### III.  Faith in oneself has no value.

Since realizing that faith finds its value externally, I no longer emphasize the "possession" of faith ("Do you have faith?"). Instead, I emphasize the perfect object of faith ("Whom do you have faith in?"). By placing my faith in Jesus, I am focusing my trust away from myself (subjective) and putting it in Him (objective). Objective faith directs our attention to Christ and away from ourselves. Read Hebrews 12:1-3 and complete the following:

"...and let us run with endurance the race that is set before us, fixing our eyes

on _____, the author and perfecter of

_____" (Hebrews 12:1,2).

Faith, focused on Christ, finds value in Him and establishes Him as the leader and perfecter of faith. The Lord Jesus demonstrated perfect faith in His Father when:

"who for the joy set before Him endured the _____,

despising the shame, and has sat down _____.
For consider Him who has endured such hostility by sinners against Himself, so

that you may not _____ and _____"
(Hebrews 12:2,3).

## IV. Faith in Christ has value.

Since our generation is given to the excesses of subjectivism, it is important that we clarify our central message. Faith is not our message—Christ is our message. I have heard it said many times, and I'm sure you have as well, that *salvation is by faith!* Those who say that may mean well, of course, but salvation is simply *NOT* by faith.

"What do you mean, Josh? You spend all this time telling us how important faith is, and now you tell us that faith doesn't save us. What do you mean, 'Salvation is not by faith'?"

If by salvation you mean a personal relationship with God through Jesus Christ, then salvation is not by faith. I believe that a person is saved by the biblical method—by grace, through faith *IN JESUS!* That's the important point. When it comes to salvation, faith must have an object—Jesus Christ. Technically, we are not saved *by* faith, we are saved by grace *through* faith—*in Jesus.* Faith is simply the arm that reaches out to receive the gift of salvation in Christ.

### How are we saved?

"But now apart from the Law the righteousness of God has been manifested, being witnessed by the Law and the Prophets, even the righteousness of God

_____ for _____

_____ ; for there is no distinction; for
all have sinned and fall short of the glory of God, being justified as a gift by His

grace _____ which is

_____" (Romans 3:21-24).

"For the demonstration, I say, of His righteousness at the present time, that He

might be just and the justifier of the one who _____"
(Romans 3:26).

"For_____;

and that not of yourselves, _____;

not as a result of works, that no one should boast" (Ephesians 2:8,9).

We are saved by grace through faith in Jesus Christ. If it were just by faith, you wouldn't need Jesus. You could save yourself. If salvation were just by faith, it would become faith in faith. You could be saved by believing in anything.

**So what is our message?**

Galatians 3:26

"For you are all sons of God _____."

Acts 16:31

"And they said, '_____,
and you shall be saved, you and your household.'"

## Conclusion

The Christian's faith is objective, finding its value in Jesus Christ. Faith is meaningful only when it is placed in Christ for salvation. We are saved by grace through faith in Jesus. The emphasis, then, is on *who* you believe rather than on simply believing.

————————O————————

**Feedback**

Complete these sentences. Refer to the key at the end of this lesson for the answers.

1. The Christian's faith is an _____ faith, not a

_____ faith.

2. Faith must have an _____ to be of any value.

3. The value of faith is not _____ but rather in

_____.

4. Salvation is not by _____. It is by grace, through

faith _____.

5. A person can be sincere, but _____.

True or False:

_____1. It doesn't matter what you believe, just so you believe it enough.

_____2. The real value in faith is the faithfulness of the one believing.

_____3. A synonym for faith is trust.

_____4. Every person has the capability to trust but that doesn't save us.

_____5. We would live chaotic lives if we didn't exercise faith.

## My Response

*Josh*

Living the Christian life is a walk of faith. Yet, I struggled for a time as a young Christian because my believing and my faith lacked true substance. I was believing creeds and doctrines while failing to fix my eyes on the author and perfecter of faith. As I began to focus on Him—His life, His nature, His Person, my faith took on value and substance.

_____

(My name)

Since my faith has no value in itself:

• In what way does my doctrine relate to the character of Christ?

• What does obedience to God's law teach me about Him?

Prayer:

*"Lord Jesus, You are the one in whom I place my faith, for You alone are worthy of my trust. It is by Your grace that You have pardoned me, and it is by faith in You that I have accepted that pardon. I praise You for being the righteous object of my faith. Amen."*

——————○——————

## For Further Reference

A popular question is: "What about those who have never heard?" Read *Answers to Tough Questions*, pages 129-134, for a usable reply.

True or False: 1. False 2. False 3. True 4. True 5. True
faith, in Jesus 5. sincerely wrong.
Completion: 1. objective, subjective 2. object 3. in the one believing, the one who is believed 4.
**KEY**

# CHRIST IS THE SOURCE
# OF GROWTH

### A Quick Look Back

I understand that the value of my faith depends upon the object of my faith for there is no worth in faith itself. In order to be saved, we must place our faith in Jesus, for we are saved, not by faith, but *by* grace, *through* faith, *in* Jesus. Faith does not save; Jesus saves. Faith is simply the arm that reaches out to receive what Christ has done for us.

———————————O———————————

### Key Truth

***The basis for Christian growth is faith in Jesus Christ.***

I will learn:

- that Christian growth begins and continues by faith in Christ.
- what I receive from Christ by faith enabling me to grow.
- that objective faith in Christ involves acceptance of His righteousness.

### What Would You Say?

"If Christianity works for you, that's fine. Everyone must seek something within him that enables him to find answers. The important thing is that you unlock that hidden reservoir or meaning that lies deep within each person. Experiencing a deep religious belief works for many, as it no doubt has worked for you. But, it's just not for me..."

What would *you* say?

I would say _____

_____

_____

Because _____

_____

_____

———————————————○———————————————

## Let's Lay A Foundation

My relationship with Christ is the basis for my spiritual growth. I grow as I know Him better, and I know Him better only by faith. Fellowship is maintained by a continued faith in Him.

Just as salvation comes through faith in Christ, so spiritual growth comes as we direct our faith to an object outside ourselves.

Continual faith in Christ is the means whereby we receive God's power to live the Christian life. This principle is seen abundantly in the Gospels and Epistles.

### I. Growth begins by faith.

Faith in Christ is the first step in the Christian life, and it is just as essential to every subsequent step we take in our walk with Christ.

1. The gospel is based on faith.

"For in it (the gospel) the righteousness of God is revealed (to us

believers) from _____ ;

as it is written, 'but the righteous man _____ ' "
(Romans 1:17).


2. We communicate with God through faith.

We see in Hebrews 11 (God's great "gallery of faith") that faith is essential for communicating with God. Take time to read the whole chapter for a look at Old Testament examples of men and women who lived by faith.

"And without faith it is _____ , for

He who comes to God must _____ , and that He

is _____ who seek Him" (Hebrews 11:6).


3. We receive from God by faith.

James leaves no doubt that faith is the only way to receive anything from God.

"But let him ask _____ ,
for the one who doubts is like the surf of the sea driven and tossed by the wind.

For let not that man _____

_____ from the Lord, being a double-minded (doubting) man, unstable in all his ways" (James 1:6-8).

## II. Growth continues by faith.

Faith in Christ is essential for Christian growth, therefore we place our faith *in Jesus*. The source of our power for growth is Christ.

What parallel is there between *becoming* a Christian and *living* a fruitful Christian life?

Colossians 2:6,7— _____

_____

_____

What key phrase does the Apostle Paul use in describing how he lived?

Galatians 2:20— _____

_____

These passages of Scripture emphasize the process of Christian growth, which takes place only as we put our faith *in Jesus*. "I live by *faith in the Son of God*," Paul said. There is no clearer way to state the importance of recognizing Christ as the source for spiritual growth.

But have you ever said, "Oh, I need more faith"? Having "objective faith" turns the focus away from how much faith I have to who that faith is in. It's not the size of my faith that matters; it's the greatness of God that matters. We don't need great faith in God; we need faith in a great God.

How much faith does Jesus say we need?

Luke 17:6— _____

_____

The disciples immediately caught the significance of Jesus' comparison of faith with a mustard seed, for the mustard seed was considered to be the smallest unit of measure. The issue is, in *whom* have we placed our faith?

## III. Growth depends upon faith.

There are many words to describe the character of God, but the word that best reflects the essence of His nature is "righteousness." Christ's righteousness, received by faith, is what causes me to grow.

As a Christian, I continually discover areas of my life that need to be aligned with Christ's righteousness. As I get to know Christ better, I submit new areas of my life to His control.

The Apostle Paul makes this major point in Philippians 3:7-9.

"But whatever things were gain to me, those things I have counted as _____

_____" (Philippians 3:7).

"More than that, I count _____

in view of the _____ for whom

I have suffered the loss of all things, and count them but rubbish in order

that _____" (Philippians 3:8).

"And may be found _____, not having

_____ derived from the Law,

but that which is through _____

_____ on the

_____" (Philippians 3:9).

In a similar vein, Paul wrote to the Corinthian church.

"But by His doing you are in Christ Jesus, who became to us _____

_____, and _____

and _____ and _____"
(1 Corinthians 1:30).

"He made Him who knew no sin to be sin on our behalf, that we might

become the _____"
(2 Corinthians 5:21).

## Conclusion

My growth as a Christian depends upon continuing to place my faith in Christ In doing so, I receive His righteousness into new areas of my life. This is trusting Him for *what* He is—the righteous God.

1. What is the basis on which I receive anything from God?

_____

_____

_____

2. In order to get God to do great things in our lives, how much faith do we need?

_____

_____

_____

3. How do you respond to the statement, "The most important thing to God is how sincere you are"?

_____

_____

_____

———————————O———————————

## My Response

*Josh*

Many times in my Christian walk I have tended to think I could somehow solve my own problems. It may seem that if people created their problems, they should be able to solve them. But, this simply is not the case. The solution is found only as I recognize Christ as my righteousness. The answers are not within, they are found in a source outside myself—the righteousness of Christ.

_____

(My name)

As I have gone through this lesson, I have recognized areas of my life which I am not trusting Christ to control. I will list these below and begin today to trust Christ for what He is—righteous.

In what specific area of my life do I want God to change me?

_____

_____

_____


The way I will begin is:

_____

_____

_____


The following is the biggest barrier to my trusting Christ for what He is:

_____

_____

_____


To more fully comprehend God's righteousness that is mine by faith, I will make this prayer my own:

> "Lord Jesus, I praise You that You are my righteousness. By faith I rely upon all that You are to make me acceptable to God. Power for living is found in Your righteousness. Thank You for giving me Your righteousness on the basis of faith. Amen."

Misconception No. 3

THE CHRISTIAN'S FAITH IS
A BLIND FAITH

# CHRIST PROVIDES REASONS

### A Quick Look Back

Christian faith is an objective faith. It must have an object. Faith has no value in itself, but only in the object in which it's placed. We are saved, not by faith, but by grace through faith in Jesus. In addition, I have learned that my growth as a Christian depends upon employing the same principle by which I first came to Christ—placing my faith in Jesus. This faith is objective, for it finds solutions in the righteous character of Christ.

───────○───────

### Key Truth

**The Christian's faith is an intelligent faith, for it provides a reason for trusting in Christ.**

I will learn:

- that faith in Christ is based on logical evidence.
- that my mind and heart were created to be in harmony with each other.
- that intelligent faith investigates the evidence for faith.
- that faith decides on the basis of the weight of the evidence.

───────○───────

### What Would You Say?

"Believing is a function of man in his search for meaning. It is not important to understand and explain the rationale of your religion, because trying to substantiate your beliefs is futile and meaningless. The important thing is that you believe, for this gives you an identity..."

What would *you* say?

I would say _____

_____

Because _____

_____

_____

### Let's Lay A Foundation

I used to think, as many do today, that the faith of a Christian is exercised blindly. But I soon learned, upon investigating Scripture, that the intellect plays a significant role in the exercise of faith. In Scripture, no one is ever called upon to exercise a blind faith.

## I. Faith uses the mind.

1. Truth and the intellect.

Based on the following passage, what place does Jesus say the intellect has in knowing truth? What are the results?

"Jesus therefore was saying to those Jews who had believed Him, 'If

you abide in My word, then you are truly disciples of Mine; and_____

_____, and_____

shall make you free' " (John 8:31,32).

Explain _____

_____

Jesus said concerning truth, "You shall *know* the truth"; that is, you will know the truth rationally and intelligently. Comprehending the truth will free us. The mind, then, is crucially important to recognizing the impact truth can make upon our lives.

2. Faith and the intellect.

Throughout his lifetime the Apostle Paul challenged believers and unbelievers to evaluate intellectually the evidence for the Messiahship of Jesus. Paul's faith in Jesus was based on what he knew was true. He often strongly reasoned with his audience, persuading them to receive Christ on the strength of the evidence he presented (Acts 18:4).

In the latter part of his life Paul testified:

"For this reason I also suffer these things, but I am not ashamed; for _____

_____

and _____ to guard what

I have entrusted to Him until that day" (2 Timothy 1:12).

What does this verse teach concerning faith and the use of the intellect?

_____

_____

_____

Faith is never a mindless act. Paul said, "I *know* whom I have believed." His knowledge of the one in whom he placed his faith sparked confidence in Christ's ability to keep his trust. Knowledge of the one in whom you place your trust is essential for a confident hope.

## II. Faith harmonizes the heart and mind.

When Jesus appealed to the intellect, He did so on the basis of the unity of man. Christ redeems the whole man: mind, will and emotions; body, soul and spirit. What I understand intellectually affects me spiritually, morally, socially and even physically. The heart and mind were created to work in harmony. The heart cannot rejoice in what the mind rejects.

1. The believing mind.

In summing up the commandments, Jesus made clear that the use of our intellect is a part of our service to God.

" 'Teacher, which is the great commandment in the Law?' And He said

to him, ' _____

_____ , and_____

_____ , and _____ .

This is the great and foremost commandment' " (Matthew 22:36-38).

There is harmony in serving God with my intellect and submitting my heart and will to Him. I serve God with my whole being.

In a parallel passage, Jesus reinforced this point by commending one of His listeners. What did Jesus say?

Mark 12:34— _____

_____

Does this show that the mind must be used in coming to Christ? If so,

explain._____

_____

59

2. The unbelieving mind.

Satan recognizes that the intellect is exercised in placing faith in Christ. What measures does He take to try to prevent this?

2 Corinthians 4:4— _____

_____

_____

_____

How does the Gospel counteract Satan's work?

2 Corinthians 4:6— _____

_____

_____

_____

## III. Faith is based on evidence.

Faith in Christ is based on evidence that can be evaluated intelligently. Jesus never asked anyone to believe in Him blindly. He always offered evidence on which to base faith.

1. Jesus offers evidence

Several Scripture passages illustrate the necessity of using the mind to evaluate evidence for the Christian faith.

What evidence did Jesus offer Thomas?

John 20:25,27— _____

_____

_____

What was John's purpose in recording evidence in his gospel?

John 20:30,31— _____

_____

_____

How were the disciples convinced of the reality of Christ's resurrection?

Acts 1:3— _____

_____

_____

2. Faith recognizes limitations.

(1) Conclusive but not definitive.

An intelligent evaluation of available evidence never means 100 percent certainty. Faith follows the direction in which the evidence points and never goes against the evidence. Although the evidence is often overwhelmingly convincing, it is never 100 percent certain. But faith decides on the basis of the weight of that evidence which makes up for the lacking percentage.

(2) Adequate but not exhaustive.

Very few things can be proven with 100 percent certainty. But that shouldn't surprise us. The evidence on which we decide is fully adequate, and elements of uncertainty cause us to exercise more care, not less. God calls us to place faith in His Son, not because we know all there is to know, but because He has given us enough knowledge on which to base our faith. So, though the evidence is not exhaustive, it is sufficient. Faith does not go against reason; it harmonizes with it by going along with the evidence. The mark of Christian faith is this, it is based upon reliable evidence.

On numerous occasions the Apostles and early Christians challenged unbelievers to see for themselves "if these things be so." Repeatedly, they urged people to weigh the evidence. The facts about Jesus were well known at the time of the Apostles' preaching, and many witnesses were available to anyone who wanted to investigate the truth. Jesus' words were spoken publicly and His works were performed openly, therefore anyone who desired to investigate their validity could do so. The challenge was not simply to believe, but to "know these things" and believe (Acts 26:26).

Intelligent faith is an assurance of the heart, resting in the adequacy of the evidence. But blind faith is believing without reliable evidence or even in spite of evidence. Faith never goes contrary to the evidence, taking a leap into the dark. Instead, it is a step into the light. A Christian's faith is exercised intelligently on the basis of evidence.

## Conclusion

We have seen that the Bible urges us to use our minds in deciding about Jesus Christ. Christianity, then, is reasonable and sensible. It involves faith based on reliable evidence. However, one does not come to Christ with the mind alone; faith must be exercised. Yet, that faith is based upon evidence, not false hope.

Without referring to the lesson, match each concept with the Scripture passage. Refer to the key at the close of the lesson for the answer.

Match references with statements:

1. 2 Timothy 1:12

2. 2 Corinthians 4:4

3. John 8:32

4. Acts. 1:3

5. Matthew 22:36-38

A. Knowing the truth will set you free.

B. Faith is knowing in whom I believe.

C. Our mind, will and emotions harmonize in serving God.

D. Satan darkens the minds of unbelievers to prevent them from evaluating the evidence.

E. Christ offered convincing proofs of His resurrection.

Fill in the key words:

1. The heart cannot rejoice in what _____.

2. "You shall _____ the truth."

3. "I _____ I have believed."

4. Intelligent faith is an assurance of the heart, resting in the _____

_____.

5. Faith decides on the basis of the _____.

6. Blind faith is believing _____.

———————————O———————————

**My Response**

*Josh*

There have been times when I have been troubled by doubts. I've asked myself, "McDowell, how do you know what you believe is true? Maybe you've been taken in by a giant propaganda program! How do you know that God exists, that the Bible is true, that miracles happened or that your faith is not just wishful thinking?" I first felt guilty that I had such thoughts, but then I was reminded that Christ never expected me to trust him blindly. He created me with a logical mind that was to harmonize with my heart. I can testify that the more closely I examine the facts the deeper my faith is rooted. I always come back to two things: the historical, objective facts of the resurrection and the internal experience of a changed life!

_____
(My name)


Here is a list of some doubts I've had recently.

_____

_____

_____

_____

_____


What are some facts that I know demonstrate God's greatness in these areas?

_____

_____

_____

_____

_____


This is my prayer:

> *"Lord Jesus, I thank You for leaving a trail of evidence for me to follow in affirming Your Lordship over my life. I'm grateful that You have given me evidence I can intelligently evaluate and hold on to. Those facts give me the basis of my faith, even when I'm under attack by Satan. Right now I reaffirm my trust in You. Amen."*

—————————O—————————

## For Further Reference

Under the section, "Believing Faith," in *Answers to Tough Questions*, read the replies to "Is it sensible to believe in Christianity?" pages 139-148, and "Does it really matter what I believe?" pages 149-151.

Also in *The Resurrection Factor*, chapter 2, "Obvious Observations," read Observation #4—Intelligent Faith. These readings will provide further amplification of intelligent faith.

KEY

Matching: A-3, B-1, C-5, D-2, E-4

Fill in: 1. the mind rejects 2. know whom 3. know 4. adequacy of the evidence 5. weight of the evidence 6. without reliable evidence.

LESSON
**8**

# CHRIST PROVIDES PURPOSE

### A Quick Look Back

I have learned that my faith in Christ is an intelligent faith. It is based on the weight of the evidence. This brings my mind and heart into harmony, for I trust Christ with my whole mind, will and emotions.

───────○───────

### Key Truth

*Intelligent faith provides meaning and purpose for my everyday circumstances, for I see how they fit into God's plan for my life.*

I will learn:

- that intelligent faith enables me to apply truth to my life.
- that everyday circumstances can be God's tools for making me become like Him.
- that faith reveals God's purpose for me.

───────○───────

### What Would You Say?

"You and I control our own destiny. God expects us to make things happen. Faith may give you peace and the freedom to find meaning for yourself, but remember, faith is a private matter. The important thing is for each person to determine his own purpose in life, hoping in some way to leave a lasting impression on the world..."

What would *you* say?

I would say _____

_____

_____

Because _____

_____

_____

—————————————O—————————————

## I. Intelligent faith provides understanding.

God invites us to ask, seek and knock. This requires the use of our minds, for He wants to share with us His intimate secrets so that we may relate truth to our everyday living.

1. Understanding requires application.

Understanding takes place when we know how to apply truth correctly. Simply knowing a truth or principle without applying it with the heart is not satisfactory.

"Who among you is wise and _____?

Let him show by his _____ his

_____ in the gentleness of wisdom" (James 3:13).

"And the one on whom seed was sown on the good ground, this is the

man who hears the Word and _____ it;

who indeed _____, and brings forth, some a hundredfold, some sixty, and some thirty" (Matthew 13:23).

According to Matthew 13:19, what happens when someone hears the Word but does not perceive how it applies?

_____

_____

Intelligent faith unites the intellectual evaluation of truth and inward perception of the heart with its application to our lives. We glorify God when our faith results in the mind and heart joining together to produce godly behavior.

2. Understanding requires association.

In some of the richest language of Scripture, Paul emphasizes that the key to understanding is knowing Christ.

"More than that, I count all things to be loss in view of the surpassing value

of _____ Christ Jesus my Lord..."
(Philippians 3:8)


"...That I may _____, and the power of His

_____ and the fellowship of His

_____, being conformed to His death..."
(Philippians 3:10).


"...that the God of our Lord Jesus Christ, the Father of glory, may give

to you a spirit of _____

and of revelation in the _____ of _____"
(Ephesians 1:17).


Understanding with our hearts and minds how truth applies depends upon our knowing Christ well. As believers, our hope is founded upon the intimacy of our relationship with Christ.

3. Understanding requires examination.

The early church leaders frequently urged believers to evaluate intelligently any doctrine they received. They gave their converts solid criteria for judging doctrine (2 Corinthians 11:4-15; Galatians 1:6-9).

A stimulating challenge to us, as believers, is the example of the Bereans. Paul and Silas preached the gospel to the Bereans, who didn't just accept this new doctrine blindly. (Read Acts 17:10-15).

What earned the Bereans a good reputation?

Vs. 11— _____

_____

_____


What was the result of their noble-minded search?

Vs. 12— _____

_____

_____

_____

The Bereans were not about to accept something just because missionaries in sandals came along and taught it! The Apostle Paul did not discourage their open-minded search by saying, "Just believe." Examining the Scriptures to understand how to apply God's truth to our own lives is the only sure way of establishing a solid foundation for our faith.

## II. Intelligent faith provides purpose (Romans 8:28-39).

Do you recall our definition of faith? Faith is the assurance of the heart, resting in the adequacy of the evidence.

Certainty about God's control comes when I intelligently submit, surrender, rest in, acknowledge and accept His work in my life. This creates a deep conviction that God does have a plan for me to follow. I am a person of destiny!

In Romans 8:28-39, God reveals His cosmic plan for all believers.

Who causes "all things" to work together?

Romans 8:28— _____

_____

_____

What does this imply about God's direct involvement in even minor details of your life? Explain.

_____

_____

_____

_____

_____

_____

What pattern is God following in His development of you?

Romans 8:29— _____

_____

_____

_____

With God on our side, how certain can we be in the face of difficulty and opposition that He will fulfill His plan?

Romans 8:30,31,37— _____

_____

_____

_____

God, who is in control of the events of every believer's life, focuses even apparently meaningless events into one meaningful purpose. His plan is to make us like His Son Jesus. He is at work in each experience and circumstance to give us the opportunity to trust intelligently in His control. And while God *does not will* adverse conditions or circumstances upon us. He is able to *use* them to achieve the goals of making us more like Christ.

## Conclusion

Intelligently understanding the basis of my faith leads to a deeper understanding of God's purpose for every circumstance I face. He does not want me to accept blindly what comes; rather, He delights in my humble search to know Him and His plan for me. When I acknowledge and submit to His sovereign control, I discover how He uses my present circumstances to create in me the family likeness of His Son. He wishes to use even mundane events as opportunities for me to trust in His control.

————————————O————————————

### Feedback

Choose the correct answer.

1. Define intelligent faith.

_____A belief in the improbable.

_____A decision based upon 100 percent certainty.

_____The assurance of the heart, resting in the adequacy of the evidence.

2. Paul and Silas commended the Bereans because they:

_____accepted without question Paul's teaching.

_____were not discouraged by hardship.

_____diligently searched the Scriptures to confirm the accuracy of Paul's teaching.

_____were close-minded.

3. God's ultimate purpose for me is to:

_____make me a missionary.

_____make me successful in my vocation.

_____develop me into the likeness of His Son Jesus.


4. The tools God uses to shape me into Christ's likeness are:

_____hours of solitude and reflection.

_____the common reversals and circumstances of life.

_____spiritual events, like Bible conferences and seminars.

_____known only by God and no one else.

───────────────○───────────────

## My Response

*Josh*

As a single, I discovered real purpose through trusting God for who I should marry. I had a great dating life (you would too if you waited till 31 to get married!) yet I wanted to wait for the perfect girl God had designed for me. By yielding to God's control over my singleness I developed self-control (which has certainly helped since). Repeatedly I had opportunity to trust God in the area of love, sex and dating. As a result, I reaped a sense of purposeful destiny. Now, I truly thank God for the beautiful wife and loving family He has provided. It's best to trust in God!

_____
(My name)


The circumstance that I find most difficult to accept as God's tool for making me like Christ is:

_____

_____

_____

_____

_____


The most significant concept I have learned in this study about God's plan for my life is:

_____

_____

_____

_____

Because of what I've learned, I plan to:

_____

_____

_____

_____

As I see God's hand in each circumstance, I will commit myself to learning that all of life's situations are opportunities to exercise a conscious trust in God's sovereign control. This, then, is my prayer based on Paul's prayer in Ephesians 1:18,19:

*"I pray that the eyes of my heart may be enlighted so that I may know*

- *what is the hope of Your calling,*

- *what are the riches of the glory of Your inheritance in me, and*

- *what is the surpassing greatness of Your power toward me as I believe."*

**KEY**

1. The assurance of the heart, resting in the evidence.  2. Diligently searched the Scriptures to confirm the accuracy of Paul's teaching.  3. Develop me into the likenes of His son.  4. The common reversals and circumstances of life.

# Misconception No. 4

# THE CHRISTIAN'S FAITH HAS NO HISTORICAL BASIS

# CHRIST VIEWS OBJECTIVELY

### A Quick Look Back

I have discovered that the Christian has an intelligent faith, for it is faith based upon evidence. Jesus never asked anyone to believe in Him blindly. He offered evidence to substantiate His claim to be God's Son. Through intelligent faith, my understanding of God's purpose and design is increased, and I become a creature of destiny as I rest in the knowledge that God is causing all things to work together for my good and His glory.

────────○────────

### Key Truth

*History provides the evidence on which my faith is based.*

I will learn:

- how modern historical research is conducted.
- how Christ's claims can be substantiated in history.
- two ways history can be interpreted.
- how to view history objectively.

────────○────────

### What Would You Say?

"You must remember, we're talking about religious history. You can't expect me to accept it just as I would the writings of Caesar or Plato. You must keep in mind that the Bible is a religious book. The authors had to expand upon the things they believed and project them bigger than life in order to impress their followers. Every religion has done this over the years. This is what causes a greater following for some religions than others..."

What would *you* say?

I would say _____

73

_____

_____

Because _____

_____

_____

——————————o——————————

## Let's Lay A Foundation

I think we all would admit that it's hard to discuss a controversial subject without being biased. "The Dallas Cowboys have the best quarterback in the NFL!" That raises some eyebrows, doesn't it? It's hard to be objective—admit it! When it comes to the historical evidence on which our faith is based, we don't have the luxury of forming our own opinion. Our examination of the evidence must be unbiased and objective. What works with football teams won't work here! We must carefully examine how we interpret history.

### I. The biblical approach to history.

Do you love history? (I can hear the groans!) Many people find history dry and boring. This is possibly due to unpleasant memories of monotonous lectures or tedious assignments in school. So they avoid anything remotely connected with history. But did you ever consider that your comprehension of God's Word is dependent upon your approach to history?

### Time-Space Dimension History

God revealed Himself in the person of Jesus Christ at a specific time and in a specific place in history. The recorded events of Jesus' life have all the marks of actual history. In other words, the events of Jesus' life took place at a specific time within the physical dimensions of space. They really happened! This is called "time-space dimension history."

List some specific reference points of time and space associated with Christ's life and ministry.

| Time | Space |
|---|---|
| Luke 2:1,2— _____ | Matthew 2:22,23— _____ |
| Luke 2:41, 42— _____ | Mark 1:9— _____ |
| Luke 3:23— _____ | Matthew 4:12-16— _____ |
| Mark 15:25, 33, 34— _____ | Matthew 27:32-36— _____ |

The evidence on which a biblical faith is based is open to historical investigation. All that Christ said and did fell into a specific place and time in history. Some recent theologians have taught that there is a special kind of "religious" history that cannot be examined as real. In their view "secular" history can be examined for its truth (Was Abraham Lincoln assassinated? Did Julius Caesar ever live?), but not "religious" history (Did Jesus of Nazareth rise from the dead?). Nothing could be further from the truth! A Christian's faith is based upon events of history, and the historical evidence supporting that faith can be examined on the same basis as other facts of history.

## II. The modern approach to history.

When I speak in a history class I usually explain that if I followed the *modern* historical approach to Christianity, I would never believe in the deity of Christ, the resurrection, or the Bible as God's Word. Note that I said the *modern* historical method. The issue is not history but the modern *approach* to history.

Modern study of history denies the supernatural, interpreting all world events as having a natural explanation.

Four major anti-supernatural presuppositions control the modern historian's investigation:

1. There is no God.

2. We live in a closed, self-causation system.

3. There are no miracles.

4. There is no supernatural.

If there is no God, then obviously God cannot be involved in our world. Miracles are not possible, because miracles are events that cannot be explained by natural, normal means.

Modern conclusions about history are based, not on historical information alone, but on philosophical prejudice. What is assumed in advance dictates the conclusion. By the tyranny of their assumptions, modern historians determine what they will find before they do their investigation. They are biased, not because of historical facts, but because of their view of the world. Because they rule out the supernatural, they interpret history through a cloud of presuppositions.

A presupposition is a conclusion assumed in advance to be true.

There are essentially two kinds of presuppositions.

1. Substantive presupposition.

This approach to historical events presupposes certain pre-conceived conclusions. The historian, working under this method, already knows the outcome of his investigation before the facts are considered. This method, used to interpret history, limits objectivity.

2. Methodological presupposition.

This method for discovering truth within history simply determines in advance the technique to be used in gathering facts about a historical event. It does not predetermine what will be found. It allows the facts to speak for themselves without trying to explain them away. Apart from this approach objectivity is impossible.

### The Platypus Story

The story of the discovery of the platypus is a classic example of the presuppositional approach to history.

Let's assume you are a modern historian who knew through many extensive and exhaustive studies that mammals do not have webbed feet and bills like ducks. You read in a travel magazine that numerous vacationers to Australia have seen semi-aquatic, egg-laying mammals with broad flat tails, webbed feet, and snouts resembling a duck's bill. Since you use the substantive presuppositional approach, what is your response?

Mark A or D for *agree* or *disagree*.

_____1. No such animal as described by the vacationers exists or ever could exist.

_____2. The vacationers are either: a) falsifying their reports; or b) ignorant of the true facts. Their reports cannot be accurate.

_____3. There were 125 eyewitnesses, including many highly respected, trustworthy scientists, but I still cannot accept their reports as true.

Now, let's assume you are an historian who takes the methodological presuppositional approach. You, too, believe the results of your extensive, exhaustive studies, and you believe no mammals have webbed feet and duck bills. When you read the vacationers' reports, what is your response?

Answer A or D for *agree* or *disagree*.

_____1. No such animal, as described by the vacationers, exists or ever could exist.

_____2. Possibly the vacationers are ignorant of the facts or have falsified their reports, but I cannot eliminate the possibility of such an animals's existence. More research must be done.

_____3. If, after thoughtful examination, many highly respected and trustworthy scientists confirm this creature's existence, I will believe there is such an animal.

The case of the duck-billed platypus illustrates the difference between these two approaches to history. When explorers returned to England after their first encounter with this strange animal, the scientific community simply refused to believe in the platypus. Why? Because of the evidence? No! They rejected the evidence because their presuppositions dictated that no mammal had webbed feet and a duck's bill. This underscores the importance of harmonizing presuppositions with facts.

## Conclusion

The evidence on which our faith is based is found in history. We examine historical reports thoroughly, determine their reliability, and base our faith upon that evidence, and we do not let philosophical presuppositions dictate our conclusions. Objectivity is necessary to historical research. The results depend upon it.

———————————————O———————————————

**Feedback**

Without referring to the lesson, fill in the following blanks. The correct answers will be found in the key at the close of the lesson.

1. God revealed Himself in the person of Jesus Christ at a specific _____

_____ , and in a specific _____ in history. The recorded events of Jesus' life have all the marks of actual history. This is

called _____ - _____ dimension history.


2. The issue is not the history but the modern _____
to history.

3. A presupposition is _____ to be true.


4. Four anti-supernatural presuppositions control the modern historian's investigation.

   1) There is _____.

   2) We live in a _____.

   3) There are _____.

   4) There is _____.

—————————O—————————

## My Response

*Josh*

One of the best things I can do for a skeptic is motivate him to check out the facts, for in the atmosphere of seeking and searching Christ will reveal Himself. As long as I held the presupposition that Christianity was intellectually indefensible, I was not receptive to truth. But when I examined the claims of Christ historically, I was brought face to face with facts that contradicted my philosophical presuppositions. I was confronted then with a decision: Would I allow *my* prejudices to reject this man who claimed to be God, or would I allow history to speak for itself? I opted to believe on the basis of the facts of history. I then submitted my will to Christ and trusted Him as Savior and Lord. I'm glad I did!


_____
(My name)


What new thought about God's work in history have I learned from this lesson?

_____

_____

_____

_____

How will this help me in my walk with Christ?

_____

_____

_____

_____


I will make this my prayer:

> *"Lord Jesus, I thank You for stepping into our time-space dimension history and revealing Yourself as the true Son of God. I am glad You have given historical evidences that ground my faith and enable me to come to know who and what You are. Amen."*

———————————O———————————

## For Further Reference

Read *More Evidence That Demands a Verdict*, chapter 1, "The Presupposition of Anti-Supernaturalism," pages 1-16, for an in-depth analysis and answer to the modern approach to history.

*The Resurrection Factor*, chapter 2, "Obvious Observations," pages 16-20, deals with the biased approach to modern history investigating evidence for the resurrection.

Popular answers to questions asked about the possibility of miracles are contained in *Answers to Tough Questions*, pages 74-81, under the section "Miracles Then and Now."

For a succinct review of the misconception covered in this lesson read *Evidence That Demands a Verdict*, pages 7-10.

To document the resurrection occurring within time-space dimension history read *Evidence That Demands a Verdict*, pages 185-189.

**KEY**

1. time, place, time-space 2. approach 3. a conclusion assumed in advance 4. no God; closed, self-causation system; no miracles; no supernatural.

# CHRIST VIEWS ACCURATELY

### A Quick Look Back

I have learned that the Christian faith is based in history. God has revealed Himself through Jesus Christ within real history. The modern approach to history denies the intervention of the supernatural into our world because of preconceived conclusions. The Christian's faith, however, is based upon historical events that can be verified the same as secular facts of history.

———————————○———————————

### Key Truth

*A biased view of God's involvement in history distorts our perception of truth and life around us.*

I will learn:

- how God views history.
- that I can accurately perceive life from God's perspective.
- the three steps for understanding God's view of history.

———————————○———————————

### What Would You Say?

"Because I don't believe in all the Old Testament miracles doesn't mean I don't believe in God. I think He uses the natural processes of nature to accomplish His purposes. He has given us minds and resources, and he expects us to use them. Just because I don't go along with all this hocus-pocus Christianity doesn't mean I don't understand God's destiny for man."

What would *you* say?

I would say _____

_____

_____

Because _____

_____

_____

———————————◯———————————

## Let's Lay A Foundation

Naturalistic scientists let their presuppositions dictate their historical conclusions. They don't objectively evaluate the facts. We often do the same thing with God's work in *our* lives! We impose a natural interpretation upon the very events God wishes to use to demonstrate His power. We don't see things accurately. But God does!

### I. God's view of history.

God has a perspective on human existence which is totally different from man's natural outlook. From His eternal viewpoint, God sees the end from the beginning.

Isaiah 55:8,9—" 'For my thoughts _____,

neither are _____,' declares the

Lord. 'For as the heavens are higher than the earth, so _____

_____,

and _____ than _____.' "

Isaiah 40:22—"It is He who _____ the

_____ of the earth."

God sees the totality, the whole. With unlimited perception and knowledge He sees all of life, whereas man's perception is very restricted. And with the modern approach to history, man's perception of history and all that is around him is distorted.

### II. Man's view of history.

An accurate view of history is based upon God's view of life. This requires an exercise of faith, for God's ways are opposite to man's natural inclinations.

There are some important principles to follow in accepting God's view of life for this does not come naturally. We need a renovation of our thought processes. We have a limited, human perspective on things. This "renewal of our minds" is done by the Word of God (Romans 12:2).

1. Choose to agree with God.

Reality is as God sees it. God has communicated His perspective to us through His Word. This must become our new "frame of reference."

After reciting the history of God's miraculous guidance of Israel (Joshua 24), Joshua challenged God's people to choose God's way.

Joshua 24:14,15—"Now, therefore, _____

and _____;

and put away the gods which your fathers served beyond the River and in

Egypt, and _____ . And if it is disagreeable

in your sight to serve the Lord, _____:

whether the gods which your fathers served which were beyond the River, or

the gods of the Amorites in whose land you are living; but _____,

_____."

What was the people's reply?

Vs. 18— _____

_____

_____

_____

Choosing to agree with God's way is the first step toward viewing all of life accurately.

2. Refuse to accept your limited perception as accurate.

This is humbling! We must actively remind ourselves that our view is not an accurate one. When we face disappointments in personal relationships, financial reversals or other disappointments, it's easy to despair. But, God's Word warns us of the fallacy of living on the basis of our limited view of the world.

Proverbs 16:25—"There _____

which _____ , but its end is the
way of death."

It is necessary to remind ourselves often that our ways and thoughts are not God's ways and thoughts.

3. Accept God's evaluation as correct.

Psalms 37:5,6—"Commit your _____ , trust

also in Him, _____ , and He will bring

forth _____ as the light, And

_____

Believing that the ways of God are best, even though our present circumstances do not seem to confirm this, is the essence of faith in God. It is also the basis of true wisdom.

## Conclusion

The modern approach to history with its anti-supernatural bias is similar to our failure to accurately see life as God sees it. By contrast, the Christian demonstrates faith and true wisdom by evaluating historical events from God's perspective. He does this as he takes three steps: (1) he chooses to agree with God; (2) he refuses to accept his own limited perception as accurate; and (3) he accepts God's way as correct.

———————O———————

### Feedback

Without referring back to the lesson, answer these True/False statements. See the Key at the end of the lesson for correct answers.

True or False:

_____1. When I think I can see accurately from within myself, it keeps me from seeking God's viewpoint.

_____2. Since I became a committed Christian, my thoughts have been the same as God's thoughts.

_____3. True wisdom is believing God's ways are best even when present circumstances seem to deny it.

_____4. Knowing that my human perspective is restricted, I place my trust in God's Word in order to see and know His ways.

———————O———————

### My Response

*Josh*

One of the main stepping stones in my walk with Christ has been the recognition that I don't see naturally from God's viewpoint. As I have placed my trust in God by acknowledging that I don't see clearly, He has revealed His way to me through my wife and friends. Prior to this faith in God's accurate perception, I persisted stubbornly in what I thought was correct. But, as I came to understand that my thoughts and ways were not His, I became open to others' views. Since then, almost without exception, He has shown me His viewpoint through the lives of those around me.

_____
(My name)

Who might God be using to show me His view of life?

_____ _____

_____ _____

_____ _____

_____ _____

What difficult circumstance have I had recently that would have been better handled by seeing it as God sees?

_____

_____

_____

_____

I will make this prayer mine:

"Lord Jesus, I want to praise You for seeing the beginning and the end. You see so perfectly. I know You are teaching me to see my life's circumstances from Your perfect viewpoint. I desire to see as You see, and I place my trust in Your eyes, in Your thoughts and in Your ways. Show me Your ways of wisdom and help me to recognize it when You work through those around me. Amen."

KEY
1. True 2. False 3. True 4. True

# Misconception No. 5

## CHRISTIANITY
## CANNOT BE PROVEN

# CHRISTIANITY CAN BE PROVEN

### A Quick Look Back

I have seen that my faith is grounded in history, supported by historical evidence. Therefore, my approach to history is critical. The modern approach precludes the possibility of the supernatural. I see that I must interpret history without prejudice, accepting God's view as accurate, choosing to agree with God's evaluation of the facts and refusing to believe my perspective as true.

—————————O—————————

### Key Truth

*Evidence for my faith in Christ can be substantiated by the legal-historical method of proof.*

I will learn:

- two different kinds of proof.
- the limitations of the scientific method.
- what the legal-historical method is based on.
- what the scientific method is based on.

—————————O—————————

### What Would You Say?

"This is an age of science, and I don't accept anything unless it's proven to me. Prove the resurrection to me scientifically! The biggest problem with religion is that its followers want us to believe without any proof. If you can't prove scientifically what you're saying, then it's just not true. If you're going to be dogmatic about Christianity, let's have some proof!"

What would *you* say?

I would say _____

_____

_____

Because _____

_____

_____

———————————————○———————————————

The one who says, "I don't accept anything until it's proven to me scientifically," faces a big problem. It would be very difficult (not to speak of inconvenient!) to consistently live by that principle. The simplest things of life sometimes defy explanation. Fireflies, electricity, aging, digesting food, flying an airplane and even falling in love involve processes not altogether understood by even Pulitzer-prize-winning scientists!

Those who insist that scientific proof is the only "true" proof are those who do not understand what scientific proof involves.

## I. Two methods of proof.

The two basic methods used to arrive at proof are the modern, scientific method (scientific proof) and the legal-historical method (legal proof). We need to understand the difference so that we may discover the type of evidence that supports our faith in Christ.

1. The scientific method.

Scientific proof is based upon demonstrating a fact by repeating an event in the presence of the person questioning the fact. It calls for duplicating the event over and over, noting and recording the results, before drawing a conclusion.

"The scientific method, however, it is defined, is related to measurement of phenomena and experimentation or repeated observation" (The New Encyclopedia Britannica, Micropedia Vol. VIII, p. 985).

The scientific method demands the use of a controlled environment (such as a laboratory) where:

(1) observation can be made.

(2) data is drawn.

(3) a hypothesis is experimentally verified.

The scientific method involves:

- observation
- gathering of data
- theorizing
- deduction
- verification of facts by repeated experimentation.

## 2. The legal-historical method.

Legal-historical proof is based upon showing that something is true beyond a reasonable doubt. That is, the truth of a matter is decided on the basis of the weight of the evidence. There must be no reasonable basis for doubt.

The legal-historical method depends upon three types of testimony:

(1) oral testimony

(2) written testimony

(3) physical testimony (exhibits).

This is the same type of evidence that is valid in a court of law. The exhibits admissible in a court case would include a gun, a bullet or an article of clothing; written testimony could include a letter or handwritten instructions or deposition; and an eyewitness report would be an oral testimony. The jury reaches a verdict on the basis of the weight of the testimony presented.

## II. Limitations of proof.

### 1. The scientific method.

Because the scientific method is based upon experimentation, it is severely limited in proving past events, and is useful only in proving repeatable events. Science cannot answer questions about a person or an event in history.

If the scientific method was the only legitimate method for proving something, you couldn't prove that you went to work this morning or that you had your lunch today! There is no way you can repeat these events in a controlled situation. So the scientific method isn't appropriate for answering questions that relate to past events.

Based on the limitations of the scientific method, do you *agree* or *disagree* that I could prove scientifically:

*Agree* or *Disagree*

_____1. Julius Caesar was the first emperor of Rome.

_____2. Patrick Henry said, "Give me liberty or give me death."

_____3. Martin Luther King was a civil rights leader.

_____4. Jesus of Nazareth was the Son of God.

_____5. John F. Kennedy was assassinated in 1963.

_____6. Jesus was raised from the dead.

2. The legal-historical method.

While the legal-historical method can provide convincing proof about the resurrection, the reliability of the Bible or the actual facts of the Christian faith, it does have its limits.

When the question is asked, "Can Christianity be proven with 100 percent certainty?" we must answer truthfully, "No." But that doesn't leave us without any proof.

The decisive question in historical research is, "What is the most *probable* explanation for the evidence at hand?" One cannot establish 100 percent certainty through legal proof, but probability puts the matter beyond any reasonable doubt.

This should not surprise us. We base nearly all our decisions on probability. A jury bases its verdict on the most logical explanation of the weight of the evidence. An auto accident or robbery cannot be repeated in a courtroom. No reasonable doubt must exist, but if the jury waited until it established 100 percent certainty before rendering a verdict, the case could not be settled!

Based upon the application of the legal-historical method, identify the error in the following commonly held opinions:

| Frequently heard statements | The error | My answer |
|---|---|---|
| "You can't prove that Jesus Christ rose from the dead. I won't believe it until I have some proof." | | |
| "If God is real, why doesn't He just come down, introduce Himself and shake hands with me? Then I'd believe in Him." | | |
| "You can't believe the Bible. Science has proven that miracles aren't possible." | | |

## Conclusion

1. Scientific proof.

The evidence supporting the faith of a Christian is based in history. Therefore, the scientific method of proof is not applicable. The scientific method can be used only to prove repeatable events, and is therefore not appropriate for dealing with matters of history.

2. Legal-historical proof.

The evidence for the faith of a Christian is based on the record of God's acts in history and on the life, death, and resurrection of Jesus Christ. The legal-historical method of proof is designed to investigate matters of history. If we wished to prove beyond a reasonable doubt that Abraham Lincoln, Thomas Jefferson, George Washington or other figures or history existed, we would apply the legal-historical method. Based upon this same method, the truth of Christianity can be established beyond any reasonable doubt. The weight of the evidence points overwhelmingly to the validity of Christ's claims and the reliability of the Scripture.

Without referring to the material you've just covered, fill in the blank spaces below. Then, to check your answers, refer to the key at the end of this lesson.

1. What are the two methods of proof?

   (1) _____

   (2) _____

2. The scientific method demands a controlled environment where:

   (1) _____

   (2) _____

   (3) _____

3. "The scientific method of proof is useful only in _____

   _____."

4. The legal-historical method depends upon three types of testimony:

   (1) _____

   (2) _____

   (3) _____

5. "Legal-historical proof is based upon showing that _____

   _____."

*True* or *false*

_____1. In science, truth is tested by experimentation.

_____2. It is reasonable to believe that religion and Christianity should be subjected to the scientific method of proof to determine their truthfulness.

_____3. One should always be 100 percent certain before making a decision.

_____4. Scientific proof is the only "true" proof.

_____5. Science can appropriately address such questions as, "Did Julius Caesar ever live?"

_____6. Using the legal-historical method, the resurrection of Jesus Christ can be proven beyond a reasonable doubt.

*Josh*

I've told people that if God could be proven scientifically, I could never know Him personally. The actual existence of any person in history, who occupied a particular space at a specific time, cannot be proven scientifically. There is enough proof through the legal-historical method to substantiate Christ's claim to satisfy the most ardent skeptic. Before becoming a Christian, part of me wanted proof and another part of me wanted an excuse to continue living as I was. I had a proud heart that didn't want to yield, and yet an empty soul that wanted to be filled. The real proof came in finding that Christ is a person. Now I'm becoming better acquainted with Him day by day!

_____

(My name)

The most significant truth I have learned in this lesson is:

_____

_____

_____

_____

_____

I want to share these concepts with the following people:

_____

_____

_____

I will make the following prayer of application my own:

*"Lord Jesus, I thank You for the written testimony of Your Word that has been so miraculously preserved for us and assures us of who and what You are. I'm grateful You have provided a way to be assured intellectually and spiritually of Your involvement in our world and in my life. You don't leave us alone to guess but You provide adequate proof of Your individual love and concern for me. My faith is strengthened as I see You as a real person whom I can know better and better each day. Amen."*

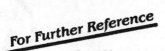

**For Further Reference**

"Can Christianity be proved?" Read *Answers to Tough Questions*, pages 145-146.

Read "What About Science?" chapter 3 of *More Than a Carpenter*, pages 36-40, for a concise explanation of the scientific and legal methods of proof.

Note also the ineffectiveness of the scientific method in refuting the evidence for the resurrection in *The Resurrection Factor*, pages 21-22.

Apply the legal-historical method to the resurrection by reading *Evidence That Demands a Verdict*, pages 189-195.

**KEY**

1. scientific proof; legal proof 2. observation can be made; data is drawn; a hypothesis experimentally verified 3. proving repeatable events 4. oral testimony; written testimony; physical testimony (exhibits) 5. something is true beyond a reasonable doubt

# CHRISTIANITY HAS BEEN PROVEN

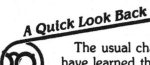
### A Quick Look Back

The usual challenge Christians receive is to prove Christianity scientifically. But I have learned that the scientific method is inadequate for proving events of history. History cannot be repeated. Nevertheless, facts of history can be proven beyond a reasonable doubt by the legal-historical method, which requires testimony.

---

### Key Truth

*Proof of Christianity through God's work in history leads me to look for specific ways in which God is at work in my life.*

I will learn:

- how to be certain of God's control of history.
- how God revealed Himself in the Old Testament.
- how God invaded history through Jesus Christ.

---

### What Would You Say?

"I don't see God doing anything spectacular today! I read of the miracles Christ performed, and of other miracles recorded in both the Old and New Testaments, and they seem like fairy tales. Did God ever reveal Himself to man? If so, doesn't He talk to us any more? Or is it just that modern man has become more knowledgeable and less open to the superstitious tales of the Bible? Besides, how could I ever know if something was a miracle? . . ."

What would *you* say?

I would say _____

_____

_____

Because _____

_____

_____

———————O———————

## Let's Lay A Foundation

The legal-historical method of proof gives us evidence of God's work in history. The historical record of Christianity, the Bible, abounds with evidence of God's might and strength. The legal-historical method proves that the Bible is actually recorded testimony of God's involvement in history. It is a record of how God has revealed Himself to man and the impact that can have on our lives.

But God is not just the God of history. He is also the God of the present, and the evidence of His past work encourages us to trust in His power for our lives right now. By faith we know He is still at work.

Based upon the evidence of history, faith also gives us hope in God's power to control the future. What an incredible sense of confidence this knowledge gives us!

What are some ways God has evidenced Himself in the past that will help us trust Him in the present?

### I. God reveals Himself in history.

On his own, man cannot know God (1 Corinthians 1:21). But God has not left us alone. He has chosen to reveal Himself. In fact, it is characteristic of God to tell us about Himself because He *wants* to be known. God is the great revealer.

How, then, does this relate to history? In this way: God's self revelation is a fact of historical record. We can be certain (on the basis of the legal-historical method) that God intervenes in history. In this sense, the Bible is God's track record! It contains the account of God revealing Himself to man. The annals of Biblical *history* are the unfolding of *His Story!*

The Bible presents, from beginning to end, God's viewpoint of history (prophecy is pre-history!). The clear message of the Bible is that God is in control. He is the Lord of history! And He demonstrates His control by managing the affairs of this world.

"The kings _____ is like _____

_____ in the _____ of the Lord: He

_____" (Proverbs 21:1).

"For God is the _____;

Sing praises with a skillful psalm. God reigns _____

_____ God sits on His _____
(Psalms 47:7-9).

95

What are some of the ways God has revealed His power over history?

1. In creation

Our Bible is a living museum of God's memoirs recorded in time. God tells *His* story. When man writes history, he usually begins with himself. When God writes history, He begins with Himself. Our first recorded view of God is in the creation of heaven and earth (Genesis 1:1). His handiwork includes the majestic craftsmanship of nature and the crown of creation, man.

What does the world of nature tell us about our creator God?

Psalms 19:1— _____

_____

_____

From Romans 1:20, what three things are clearly seen in God's historical work of creation?

1. His _____ _____.

2. His _____ _____.

3. His _____ _____.

What practical effect does this have on those who refuse to acknowledge God?

_____

_____

_____

_____

God created man in His own image (Genesis 1:27; 5:1). What inward recognition does man have about God's existence and requirements?

Romans 2:14,15— _____

_____

_____

_____

The evidence of God's power and authority in nature is termed natural revelation. However, nature does not describe God's *character*. The information we receive from creation about God is inconclusive. We need much more. Yet, in the world around him, man has a constant reminder of God's personal involvement.

2. In the lives of His people.

The changed lives of God's people is a powerful witness to God's power within history. Jesus Christ changes lives! Yet, believers are not without struggles. Unbelievers readily identify with those Christians who honestly admit their struggles. And God has given us a significant library of instruction in the past history of His people.

For what purpose were the experiences of God's people recorded in the Old Testament?

1 Corinthians 10:6,11— _____

_____

_____

_____

1 Corinthians 10:1-12 recounts several historical incidents from the Old Testament.

What are some of the lessons to be learned from these accounts of God's involvement in history? Discover and list as many as you can.

1 Corinthians 10:6-12— _____

_____

_____

_____

Reflect on what this tells you of God's control of history. Jot down any insights you may have for later use and sharing.

| Scripture reference | My insights |
|---|---|
| _____ | _____ |
| _____ | _____ |
| _____ | _____ |
| _____ | _____ |
| _____ | _____ |

The proof of God's faithfulness is found within history. The testimony of God's people inspires a wholehearted confidence in God's integrity. God has repeatedly demonstrated His commitment to keep His Word. God's consistent faithfulness to the saints of the past is proof of His self-revelation.

## II. God reveals Himself in Christ.

The greatest historical evidence of God's self-revelation is the incarnation of Jesus Christ. Through flesh and blood, God shows us what He is like. God gives us specific information about Himself through His Son. He shows us His love, mercy, justice and anger. Jesus said, "He who has seen Me has seen the Father" (John 14:9). The Son is the visible expression (Word) of God.

John 1:1,2—"In the beginning was the _____, and the

_____, and the _____

_____. _____ was in the

beginning with _____."

Vs. 14—"And the _____, and dwelt

among us, and we _____,

glory as of the _____ from the Father,
full of grace and truth."

Colossians 2:9,10—"For in Him all the _____ dwells

in bodily form, and in Him you have been _____

and He is the head over all _____."

Jesus Christ is a man of history. The legal-historical method gives us concrete evidence about this man. His life, character and work can be examined in history, based upon the testimony of His contemporaries. Any knowledge we have about past events is based upon testimony about those events. In fact, I like to define history that way: a knowledge of the past based upon testimony.

Think about it a moment. How do you know Julius Caesar ever lived? Socrates? Alexander the Great? We know about these men because we have been left historical records attesting to their existence, deeds, failures and successes.

This is the same kind of proof available to us about Jesus Christ. The New Testament is the historical (written) testimony of those who recorded eyewitness accounts or who were themselves eyewitnesses of God's revelation through Jesus Christ.

The ultimate purpose of this historical record is "that you may believe that Jesus is the Christ, the Son of God; and that believing you may have life in His name" (John 20:31). God has revealed Himself through Jesus Christ to prepare the way for you and me to have fellowship with Him. Jesus showed us God's love by coming into the world as a person—the God-man. This corresponds to the reason God depends upon you and me to be His agents in the world—to represent His love to others (2 Corinthians 5:18-20).

## Conclusion

God is the controller of history. He has chosen to demonstrate His power through creation, the lives of His people and through Jesus Christ. The evidence on which our faith is based is found within history. Proof for my faith is based upon the evidence of history through the legal-historical method of proof.

————————O————————

## Feedback

Indicate whether you *agree* or *disagree* with the following statements. (A or D)

_____1. According to Romans 1:20, nature provides us with sufficient revelation about God for *everyone* to know Christ.

_____2. When God took on flesh, He showed us exactly what He is like.

_____3. History can be defined as the knowledge of the past based upon testimony.

_____4. The past experiences of God's people stand as warnings and examples to us not to repeat the same errors.

_____5. The basis of the Christian faith—Christ's claims and His resurrection—can be proven beyond a reasonable doubt according to the legal-historical method.

————————O————————

## My Response

### Josh

My father was the town alcoholic. As a youngster I was constantly embarrassed by the jokes my friends made about my father, who often passed out in the gutter from a night of drinking. My mother died from a broken heart because of my dad. Soon after I accepted Christ, my father came to visit me and asked, "Son, how can you love a father like me?" I said, "Dad, six months ago, I hated you. But now, God's love through His Son Jesus Christ has inundated my life. By His power I can truly say, I love you." I had the joy of leading my father to Christ 45 minutes later. And his life changed before my eyes. He instantly lost his appetite for alcohol. And before his death 6 months later (due to 45 years of drinking) he had led hundreds of businessmen in our community to Christ. Christ changes lives!

_____

(My name)

How has God placed me in a strategic position for revealing Himself through me? ___

_____

_____

_____

God has worked in the past, and He is working in the present, too. What are some ways He is making Himself known to me now?

_____

_____

_____

My prayer is:

*"Lord Jesus, I praise you for revealing Yourself to me, through Your coming to earth, and Your Word. I know You plan for me to become like You, so that I can make Your glory known to those around me. I want to honor You by making Your name known. Amen."*

―――――――――O―――――――――

## For Further Reference

Discover the evidence of God's power in history to change lives. Read "The Uniqueness of the Christian Experience," chapter 12 of *Evidence That Demands a Verdict*, pages 325-367.

Apply the legal-historical method of proof to evidence for the resurrection. Read *The Resurrection Factor* and discover how evidence, presented as in a court of law, supports the biblical account of the resurrection.

# SUMMARY

# THINK IT THROUGH AGAIN!

### A Quick Look Back

I have learned that the scientific method of proof is inadequate for examining past events. However, the legal-historical method provides convincing proof of God's revelation through Jesus Christ and His control over history. The basis of the christian faith—Christ's claims and His resurrection—can be proven beyond a reasonable doubt according to the legal-historical method.

———————○———————

### Key Truth

***Knowing Christ is the basis for being able to answer why I believe.***

I will learn:

- that a Christian's faith is placed in a person, not in a set of beliefs.
- that a Christian's faith is an objective faith.
- that a Christian's faith is an intelligent faith.
- that a Christian's faith is based upon the reality of history.
- that a Christian's faith is based upon the proof of history.

———————○———————

### What Would You Say?

"Christianity may be okay for you, but it's just not for me. Jesus was a good teacher and all, and I admire Him, but I don't think it matters so much what you believe as long as you're sincere.

Besides, faith is a very personal, private matter and it's not something you can rationalize. You just believe; you don't need any proof. If you were going to try to prove your religion, you'd have to prove it scientifically because that's the only kind of real proof there is!"

What would *you* say?

I would say _____

_____

_____

Because _____

_____

_____

——————————○——————————

## Let's Lay A Foundation

This lesson will give you an opportunity to review what you've studied in this Growth Guide—some of the reasons we have hope in Christ. This does not mean you are an authority on evidences for your faith. Nor does it mean you are able to answer every possible question asked you (although you now have answered a bunch of them!). But by now you have a much better reason to give as to why you believe. You recognize that your ability to answer why you have hope in Christ is based upon how well you know Him.

This last study is designed to help you remember where you've been and to challenge you to new growth and possibilities for the future. Consider again each of the five common misconceptions of Christianity and the corresponding truth about Christ that resolves that misconception. Check the key at the end of the lesson for your answers.

### I. Misconception #1 – Christianity is a system of beliefs.

The truth about Christ that answers this misconception is:

He is my _____; I _____.

1. Christ is a person.

There are many ways to get to know a person. But the best way is to know him as a friend, conversing in a casual way and listening to what he says about himself. Review what Jesus says about His identity. Consider what that means to you.

| Scripture | I am: | What that means to me |
|---|---|---|
| (Example)<br><br>John 6:48 | The bread of life | My spiritual nourishment comes from Jesus Christ |
| John 10:9 | | |
| John 10:14 | | |
| John 14:6 | | |
| John 15:1 | | |

Complete the following summary statement about Lesson 2:

I have learned that my faith is not in a _____

but in the _____ . This is because Christ

wants to have a _____ with me.

2. Christ has a position (equal with God).

Match the passage to summary statement on the deity of Christ.

| Scripture | | Summary |
|---|---|---|
| 1. John 5:17,18 | A. | Christ forgave sins which only God could forgive. |
| 2. John 8:48-59 | B. | Christ was crucified for *being* God, not for *doing* wrong. |
| 3. Mark 2:5-12 | C. | Jesus called God "My Father," making Himself equal with God. |
| 4. Mark 14:60-64 | D. | Jesus identified Himself as "I Am," God's name in the Old Testament. |

Complete this summary statement.

If Jesus is not God, then He is unable to _____

_____ is based. Since He is God, He is able to

_____ my sins.

3. Christ is my provider/protector.

What two practical benefits do I enjoy when I submit to Christ's authority over my life?

1. _____

2. _____

How does this help me in my relationship with others?

_____

_____

_____

_____

## II.  Misconception #2 — The Christian's faith is a subjective faith.

The truth about Christ that answers this misconception is:

He is my _____ ; I _____ .

1. Christ is the object of faith.

Jot down a brief reminder of what was said under the four main headings of Lesson 5.

1. Faith in itself, has no value _____

_____ .

2. Faith in an object, has value _____

_____ .

3. Faith in oneself, has no value_____

_____.

4. Faith in Christ, has value _____

_____.

Complete this summary statement.

I have learned that faith finds its value in the _____

_____. Therefore, salvation is by _____

through _____ in _____.

2. Christ is the source of growth.

What similarity exists between becoming a Christian and growing as a Christian? What essential principle must be consistently applied in every area of the Christian walk?

_____

_____

_____

_____

_____

Complete this summary verse from Lesson 6:

"But by His doing you are in Christ Jesus, who became to us

_____, and _____,

and _____ and _____"
(1 Corinthians 1:30).

## III. Misconception #3 — The Christian's faith is a blind faith.

The truth about Christ that answers this misconception is:

He is my _____; I _____.

1. Christ provides reasons.

Match each concept with the key Scripture.

1. John 8:32         A.    Christ offered convincing proofs of His resurrection.

2. 2 Timothy 1:12

                    B.    Knowing the truth will set you free.

3. Matthew 22:36-38   C.    Satan darkens the minds of unbelievers to prevent them from evaluating the evidence.

4. Acts 1:3

                    D.    Our mind, will and emotions harmonize in serving God.

5. 2 Corinthians 4:4   E.    Faith is knowing in whom I believe.

Complete this summary statement:

I have learned that my faith is an _____ faith that

decides on the basis of the _____ of the _____.

This brings my _____ and _____ into harmony.

2. Christ provides purpose.

Provide the missing reference for each passage quoted in support of the following outline points from Lesson 8.

(1) Understanding requires application.

_____ _____:_____—"Who among you is wise and understanding? Let him show by his good behaviour his deeds in the gentleness of wisdom."

(2) Understanding requires association.

_____ _____:_____—"That I may know Him, and the power of His resurrection, and the fellowship of His sufferings, being conformed to His death;"

(3) Understanding requires examination.

_____ _____:_____—"Now these were more noble-minded than those in Thessalonica, for they received the word with great eagerness, examining the Scriptures daily, to see whether these things were so."

Based upon Romans 8:28-37, complete this summary sentence:

I have learned that intelligent faith enables me to understand God's _____ for my _____ — to make me like His Son. I am able to rest in the fact that all things _____ _____ .

## IV. Misconception #4 — The Christian's faith has no historical basis.

The truth about Christ that answers this misconception is:

He is my _____ ; I _____ .

1. Christ views objectively.

What prohibits modern historians from objectively interpreting history? Define this.

Name the four presuppositions that control the modern approach to history.

1. _____

2. _____

3. _____

4. _____

2. Christ views accurately.

_____
_____
_____
_____
_____
_____

What three steps must we take to implement God's view of history?

(1) _____

(2) _____

(3) _____

Complete this summary sentence:

I have learned that I must not interpret history with _____

_____ , but I must accept

God's view as _____ .

## V. Misconception #5 — Christianity cannot be proven.

The truth about Christ that answers this misconception is:

He is my _____ ; I _____ .

1. Christianity can be proven.

   How do you respond to the demand, "Prove to me scientifically that Jesus rose from the dead and I'll believe"?

   Complete this summary sentence:

   I have learned that _____ proof is inadequate for establishing the historical facts of my faith, but

   _____ establishes a fact beyond a reasonable doubt.

2. Christianity has been proven.

   Agree or disagree with what was said in Lesson 12 about the following subjects. How does this demonstrate God's control of history?

   *Agree or Disagree*

   _____1. God's creation is a constant reminder of His involvement in history.

   _____2. The experience of God's people is an example of how we can avoid the pitfalls of sin.

   _____3. The incarnation of Christ is historical proof of God's self revelation.

110

Complete this summary statement:

I have learned that Christ's claims can be substantiated in _____

_____ history.

My faith in Him is certain because God has demonstrated His_____

_____ .

————————O————————

## Conclusion

Summarize in one paragraph what you have learned through this Growth Guide.

_____

_____

_____

_____

_____

————————O————————

**Feedback**

List at least four people with whom you would like to share some key concept learned in these studies.

1. _____     3. _____

2. _____     4. _____

Quote the Key Verse of this Growth Guide.

1 Peter 3:15—" _____

_____

_____

_____ ."

## My Response

*Josh*

It has been a thrill sharing this time together with you. Writing this Growth Guide has deepened my conviction to be a far better husband and father before I ever become a better communicator of the gospel. My ability to minister to my wife and three children is determined by how well I know Christ. And knowing Christ has given me a deep sense of hope! My future is in the hands of a sovereign God who loves me!

_____

(My name)

What have I learned about Jesus Christ that has helped me know Him better?

_____

_____

_____

What applications have I made that will aid me in following Him?

_____

_____

_____

In what areas do I still need to grow so that I can obey Him more completely?

_____

_____

_____

Based upon Psalms 139:23,24, I will pray:

> *"Search me, O God, and know my heart; Try me and know my anxious thoughts; And see if there be any hurtful way in me. And lead me in the everlasting way. Amen."*

**KEY**

I. authority, follow Him; system of beliefs, person of Christ, personal relationship; fulfil the hope on which my faith, forgive me; provision; protection.

II. Righteousness, live through Him; object in which it's placed, grace, faith, Jesus; wisdom, righteousness, sanctification, redemption.

III. ultimate resource, receive from Him; 1-B, 2-E, 3-D, 4-A, 5-C; Intelligent, weight, evidence, heart, mind; James 3:15, Philippians 3:10, Acts 17:11; purpose, life, work together for good.

IV. wisdom, perceive through Him; no God, closed self-causation system, no miracles, no supernatural; choose to agree with God, refuse to accept your limited perception as accurate. Accept God's evaluation as correct; prejudice, accurate.

V. controller, am directed by Him; scientific, legal-historical proof; time-space dimension history, control in history.

112

# GLOSSARY

ABSOLUTE(s): An ultimate standard by which moral values are judged.

ANTI-SUPERNATURALISM: A predetermined disbelief in God's intervention in the natural order of the universe. MEV/3

APOLOGETICS: A defense of the truth. In Christian doctrine it is a logical presentation of reasons and facts that show Christianity is the true and only religion of God. EV/1

BLIND FAITH: An exercise of trust unsupported by or in spite of evidence or facts. EV/3

CHRISTIAN EVIDENCES: The facts and truths of history, science, and personal experience that substantiate the validity of the Christian faith. A sub-division of Christian apologetics. EV/1

CLOSED, SELF-CAUSATION SYSTEM: A principle of anti-supernaturalism which states that the system of the universe is closed to any outside interference by an alleged God and therefore every event within it has a natural explanation. MEV/5

CREDULITY: A disposition to believe without sufficient reason or evidence. EV/4

EXISTENTIAL/EXISTENTIALISM: Relating to moment by moment human experience. In philosophy, a world view that life is absurd and chaotic, thereby stressing that individuals must create order and meaning out of life by making their own choices.

HYPOTHESIS: An unproven assumption confirmed or unconfirmed by scientific experimentation.

INTELLIGENT FAITH: An exercise of trust evaluated by the mind and based upon adequate evidence. EV/2

LEGAL-HISTORICAL PROOF: Evidence based on showing something is fact beyond a reasonable doubt. Depends upon written testimony, oral testimony, and exhibits to demonstrate the reasonableness of the verdict. MTC/38

OBJECTIVE: That which is real independent of my personal perception. An external object that possesses reality outside myself.

PRESUPPOSITION: A conclusion that is assumed or supposed in advance to be true. MEV/3

SCIENTIFIC PROOF: Evidence based on showing something is a fact by repeating the event in the presence of the person questioning the fact. Based upon observation, the gathering of data, and experimental verification of a theory. MTC/37

SUBJECTIVE: That which is inward, personal, and relates to individual experience.

TIME/SPACE DIMENSION HISTORY: That which has actually taken place within the realm of reality and existence open to investigation as a reportable event. MEV/12

WORLD VIEW: A comprehensive conception of human existence from a specific standpoint. The framework in which a person interprets reality. MEV/3

Reference Key:

     EV — "Evidence That Demands a Verdict"

     MEV — "More Evidence That Demands a Verdict"

     MTC — "More Than a Carpenter"

(EXAMPLE: MTC/37. MTC means "More Than a Carpenter"
              /37 means the page in the book that discusses that subject.)

# When you're searching for answers
# HERE'S LIFE

## Receive it!

**Josh McDowell offers with clarity and insight, persuasive evidence confirming the absolute reliability of God's Word.**

**REASONS**—Why Skeptics Ought to Consider Christianity • Tough academic questions are often directed at Christians by skeptics. This new work from Josh McDowell delves into such current issues as biblical infallibility, and the creation versus evolution debate. Christian students, their parents and educators alike will find this book invaluable. **Reasons** will enable the reader to arrive at the truth by intelligently evaluating the various alternatives presented.

**THE RESURRECTION FACTOR**—Here is comprehensive and compelling evidence for the resurrection of Jesus Christ. From multitudes of historical documents and in depth research comes a resounding positive answer to the question ... "Can the resurrection be proven beyond any reasonable doubt?" The author presents the overwhelming facts of this supernatural event.

**ANSWERS**—To tough questions skeptics ask about the Christian faith • A highly practical reference tool, full of proven, authoritative answers to perplexing questions. It will become indispensable as a resource book in the library of any serious student, layman or pastor.

**Available now at your Christian bookstore.**

# HERE'S LIFE PUBLISHERS
### P.O. BOX 1576 · SAN BERNARDINO, CA 92402